JOURNEY HOME

ESSAYS ON LIVING & DYING

DAN GAFFNEY

National Times Media Pty Ltd
12 Plains View Crescent
Mount Riverview NSW 2774
Australia

Copyright © by Dan Gaffney 2019

The moral right of Dan Gaffney to be identified as the author of this work has been asserted.

All rights reserved. Without limiting the rights under copyright above, no part of this publication shall be reproduced, stored in or introduced into a retrieval system, or transmitted in any form or by any means (electronic, mechanical, photocopying, recording or otherwise), without the prior permission of both the copyright owner and the publisher of this book.

Cataloguing-in-Publication entry is available from the National Library of Australia: http://catalogue.nla.gov.au/

Title:	Journey Home
Subtitle:	Essays on Living and Dying
Author:	Gaffney, Dan (1962–)
ISBN:	978-0-6487122-0-6 (paperback)
	978-0-6487122-1-3 (ebook – epub)
	978-0-6487122-2-0 (ebook – mobi)
Subjects:	BODY, MIND & SPIRIT: Inspiration & Personal Growth; SOCIAL SCIENCE: Death & Dying; Disease & Health Issues; Essays
Web:	yourjourneyhome.com.au

The author has made every effort to ensure that the information in this book was correct at the time of publication. However, the author and publisher accept no liability for any loss, damage or disruption incurred by the reader or any other person arising from any action taken or not taken based on the content of this book.

Cover design by ronnoco.com.au

For my parents, Frank and Eunice,
and my children, Marcus and Hannah.

Foreword

> *Thus shall ye think of all this fleeting world: a star at dawn, a bauble in a stream;*
>
> *a flash of lightning in a summer cloud, a flickering lamp, a phantom, and a dream.*
>
> *The Diamond Sutra* [1]

Death trails our lives as surely as night follows day, but many of us still feel shocked when the news comes that we or a loved one has a life-ending ailment. Suddenly, life is shorter than we'd anticipated—its certain course suddenly truncated, pared back to something less than our imaginings.

First comes the body blow. Then the shock and awe. Life's truth delivered: I will die. Someone I love or care for will die. For real. Then, more feelings will flood in. Maybe anger or fear, and in time, some version of sadness or grief will settle in for the death-ride.

These feelings are the residue of a deep-seated notion in our culture that death is something that befalls others, not me, not mine—or not now, at least.

Often, the next visceral impulse is to ask ourselves, what can we do to avoid a death sentence? It's a question as old as humanity, reflected in our myths and religions that are awash with tales of immortality.

The lesser cousin to our dreams of immortality is this: maybe we can cheat death. Not forever, but for a little longer perhaps.

Maybe we can put off death by extending the human lifespan beyond its natural limits.

Since the middle of the last century, the use of drugs, technologies and surgical wonders has seen people with terminal illnesses live for months, sometimes years, longer than people in similar circumstances just a few generations ago.

Faced with a choice between certain death and the promise of more time, or a miracle cure, few of us can resist the yearning to live. But the possibility of more time held out by modern medicine is a fantasy of a life merely interrupted by a few extra visits to the doctor and a few more pills each day.[2]

Many people with life-ending diseases hope or imagine that life-extending therapies will give them more time to live the life that didn't seem so pressing or important until now. But the experience of many who choose death-defying medical interventions isn't what they'd imagined.

While the impact of forestalling death is unpredictable for an individual, a growing body of evidence shows many people reap a terrible bounty when they choose interventions aimed at granting them more time.

The evidence shows that they endure more illness, more complications, more depression and less autonomy than people who choose palliative and hospice care.

They're also more likely to die in an intensive care ward of a hospital, tethered to tubes and machines, in a place with little privacy that imposes a regimen of incessant disruption.

The surgeon and author Atul Gawande said, 'When there is no way of knowing exactly how long our skeins will run … our every impulse is to fight, to die with chemo in our veins or a tube in our throats or fresh sutures in our flesh. The fact that we may be shortening or worsening the time we have left hardly seems to register.'[3]

Foreword

Western culture tends to view death as a fearful and traumatic event—something to be thwarted at any cost. But in our efforts to outflank mortality we seem to be losing sight of what dying asks of us, and what we might gain as individuals and as a society.

Embracing mortality might be our opportunity to pursue and celebrate the preciousness of life; to live fully in the time we have remaining; and to review and complete the unfinished business we've accrued and deferred for too long.

But that's not all. Living with an open-hearted acceptance of death, whether our time is near or far, could be a way to craft a life-affirming legacy for our families and loved ones that's nearly unimaginable in today's world. It could also be a path to reclaim a richness we've been denied in our death-phobic culture.

Journey Home is a set of essays about living and dying with an open heart that offers a provocation—that the way we live and die could rekindle a long-forgotten memory that embodies what is timeless and deathless.

Our children and all who remember us will feed at the table we've set. Given this, we have an opportunity to nourish ourselves and everyone we touch by cultivating a willing embrace of the cycle of life and death.

Dan Gaffney
November 2019

Contents

Foreword vii
1. A stranger among us 1
2. Longer lives, predictable deaths 4
3. Averting death 8
4. Surviving the odds 13
5. Testing new therapies 16
6. Uncertainty 19
7. If we can, we should 30
8. Youth and ageing 35
9. The tyranny of hope 40
10. Annihilation 47
11. A year to live 52
12. Grief 55
13. Desire 58
14. Reciprocity 63
15. Private myths, public dreams 69
16. Homeless 73
17. The road from Damascus 78
18. White Helmets 83

19. Initiation 87
20. Identity 93
21. Living our deepest truth.................................... 99
22. Pain and suffering 103
23. No mud, no lotus 107
24. End-of-life conversations 112
25. Competence... 116
26. Euthanasia 121
27. Orphan wisdom 128
28. Unfinished business 137
29. Ars moriendi 140
30. Rituals of the body... 142
31. Ars vivendi 148
Afterword 150
Acknowledgments 154
Resources and inspiration....................................... 156
Credits 159
Endnotes... 162

A stranger among us

Few of us welcome the prospect of dying and death, mostly because our ideas are coloured by feelings of fear and dread. Regrettably, death and dying are taboos that too few of us feel ready to approach, even though they are inescapable facts of life.

Death comes to all living creatures, but despite being an everyday event, few outside the medical or funeral industries have witnessed or cared for a dying or dead person.

Yet only two generations ago it was common for families to care for their loved ones in their time of dying, often at home. In those days, dying wasn't a rumoured or fearful event that happened elsewhere. It was something our grandparents' generation witnessed and experienced in real and intimate ways.

But today, dying and death are strangers to us. In Western countries, half of us die in a hospital and another third die in residential settings like nursing homes and hospices.

The institutionalisation and medicalisation of dying mean that less than 15 per cent of people die at home, even though most of us would prefer to if we could. Since the middle of the last century we have slowly conspired to make dying and death secluded medical experiences.

In an article titled 'Bringing our dying home: how caring for someone at end of life builds social capital and develops compassionate communities', its authors wrote: 'The concept of a good death has been superseded by the concept of a managed death, one that requires professional support and knowledge ... and takes place in a hospital, or more rarely a hospice, resulting in modern death becoming "cellular, private, curtained, individualised and obscured".'[4]

This is not to suggest that dying at home among our friends and family is necessarily better than dying in a hospital or hospice setting. It's possible to have a 'good death' (however we define it) in a hospital/hospice setting and a 'bad death' at home.[5]

But even a good death doesn't come easily. Dying makes huge physical, financial, logistical and emotional claims on dying people and their families. It almost never goes the way we planned or imagined. And it never arrives on schedule. Some deaths take an eternity, often testing the good will and patience of carers and families. Others happen in the blink of an eye—before we get to say goodbye, our heartfelt words withheld too long.

But that's not all. This new phenomenon in human affairs—the removal of death and dying from our homes and families—is slowly eroding our affinity and kinship to events that have been seminal to culture since the dawn of humanity.

And there's plenty of evidence—in the form of human misery—to suggest that this conspiracy among us shrinks our capacities to be fully human, to make a meaning from death, and to die well.

In his seminal book, *Die Wise: A Manifesto for Body and Soul*, Stephen Jenkinson notes that during his time as a social worker who counselled dying people and their families, the most frequent request made of him was to talk about meaning at the end of life.

Behind this appeal is a suggestion that life and death's meanings are 'elusive or even fugitive' to us, says Jenkinson. That the meaning of our lives and deaths are riddles, mysteries, even to ourselves, that need deciphering.[6]

Jenkinson says the meaning of our life and death isn't

something we find or discover but something we *make* by being keen observers. As humans, our task is to make a meaning of life and death by acknowledging something profoundly simple.

'Life must proceed', he says, 'as if certain things must be: like life has to continue, not *you* have to continue. That life is not your lifespan or your children's lifespan, or the lifespan of what you hold dear. How about holding dear the fact that nothing you hold dear lasts?

'How about holding that close to your bosom?'[7]

Longer lives, predictable deaths

> *Ageing, for that part of each of us that identifies with an agile body and an unforgetful mind, is loss.*
>
> Stephen Levine, *A Year to Live* [8]

For most of the past hundred thousand years, life was a short and brutal affair for humans. During that epoch, an average human lifespan was barely 30 years.

One in three infants typically died in childbirth or failed to reach their first birthday. Even when a child survived infancy, he or she would see the death of many siblings and often one or both parents. Infectious diseases like measles, influenza, smallpox, cholera, typhoid, malaria and plague claimed most lives. Malnutrition, homicide, accidents and wars accounted for the rest.

At the beginning of the 20th century, one in four people in the West died before the age of five, mainly from infectious diseases, and old age was still rare—less than five per cent of people lived past the age of 85.

A century later, this pattern has reversed itself. Today, less than one per cent of deaths occur before age five, and on average 40 per cent of people die after the age of 85, largely from chronic diseases.

What changed?

First, advances in public health measures like immunisation, clean drinking water, refrigeration, lower smoking rates, random alcohol breath testing, seatbelt legislation and massive improvements in workplace safety have prevented millions of premature deaths from infectious diseases, heart attacks, strokes, cancers and injuries.

Second, medical advances such as antimicrobial infection control, vaccine development, safe blood transfusions, the discovery and widespread use of pharmaceuticals, new surgical techniques, organ transplantation, and diagnostic and treatment technologies have saved the lives of millions who would otherwise have died, or died younger.

In the past hundred years, human life expectancy at birth increased by 30 years, but the average age of death has barely budged, still hovering around 85 years.

Life expectancy at birth rose dramatically because more infants and children survived their early years and less middle-aged people were dying from lifestyle diseases like coronary heart disease and strokes. But given a relatively fixed maximum human lifespan and an increasing average life expectancy, many more people are living long enough to die in old age.

But ageing isn't for wimps. Getting old usually means acquiring a chronic disease or a disability like cancer, heart disease, musculoskeletal ailments like arthritis, or a brain- and mind-related disorder such as dementia.

So, a person who lives to the traditional retiring age of 65 in an industrialised country can expect to live more than half their remaining years with a chronic health issue that will diminish their quality of life.

But not all chronic diseases are the same. People living with cancer, for instance, often survive for many years with a relatively high quality of life before they experience a short period of decline and death.

By contrast, people with chronic heart and lung diseases often lose some of their capacity and they function more slowly, usually with recurring periods of serious illness before they die.

Different again are physically frail people, and those with brain-related diseases such as dementia and Parkinson's disease who often experience long periods of poor life quality before they die.

Across the globe, higher life expectancy and the transition of the baby-boomer generation into older age is seeing a rapid rise in the number of old people living with chronic conditions.

And in the next quarter-century, changes in life expectancy will see a doubling in the number of people who die each year. This phenomenon is creating a demographic groundswell of people who are interested in quality-of-life issues as they make the long march into an extended old age before their decline and death.

What do older people want from life?

Surveys tell us they want to maintain or improve their physical comfort and competence, their autonomy, and their dignity. They want to engage in meaningful activities and relationships, and they want to feel safe from harm or misadventure.

Said another way, many people are living long enough to become more interested in adding vitality, meaning and life to their years rather than merely adding more years to their life.

And faced with many long years ahead, many middle-aged and older people are feeling their consciousness pricked by larger existential concerns. Ageing can be a time for shedding the ego before death claims us.[9] There's plenty of evidence, for example, that older people are less interested in power and prestige than finding meaning through love and service.[10]

Getting older is also a time when we feel a greater pull to spend time with our family and friends, by volunteering, and by giving back in material and practical ways. And all the while, the decline and death of our parents, spouses and old friends bring death and dying into constant view.

Where will I go when I die? Who am I, really? What's my purpose in my remaining years? Am I truly happy?

These queries centre on an old question that comes to us from the ages: *Will I find my lotus before winter?*

Averting death

> *To most people, death remains a hidden secret, as eroticized as it is feared. We are irresistibly attracted by the very anxieties we find most terrifying; we are drawn to them by a primitive excitement that arises from flirtation with danger. Moths and flames, mankind and death--there's little difference.*
>
> Sherwin Nuland, *How We Die: Reflections on Life's Final Chapter* [11]

No dying person who loves life would choose death given the opportunity to live longer, would they?

The cultural answer to this in the West is a resounding 'no'. So, our desire for more life, even at the end of life, has driven us to make a multitude of ways to avert death in our effort to preserve our love of living.

The result is that people with terminal conditions can call on a growing array of interventions aimed at killing disease, or at the very least, adding to their remaining days.

Surgery, radiotherapy, organ and stem cell transplants, chemotherapy, blood-thinning and cholesterol-lowering drugs are among dozens of therapies that promise cure, remission or more time among the living.

Do they work? In the world of evidence-based medicine, researchers answer this question by doing clinical trials to study the effects of therapy on one group of people compared to the effects of non-treatment or a different treatment in a second, equivalent group.

In an ideal research setting, patients with a terminal condition like late-stage lung cancer are randomly assigned to either treatment or a non-treatment/different treatment group.

Distributing or randomising patients this way helps the quality and robustness of research findings by equally distributing all known and unknown factors that could affect the outcome of the study. In studies of people with terminal conditions, researchers often follow patients' progress to the point of death, usually by comparing average survival periods of each patient group, as well as any side effects of treatment.

But here's the thing: some people, when faced with a terminal disease, choose palliative or hospice care instead of seeking a cure or more time.

The purpose of palliative care is to accommodate people's physical, social, spiritual and emotional needs for any health issue, not just terminal diseases.

For those with a *terminal* condition, palliation's goal is neither to prolong life nor hasten death, but to maximise people's *quality* of life as they move towards death.

But there's a widespread belief in the community and among some healthcare providers that palliation hastens death because patients forgo curative treatment and often have access to high-dose opioids and sedatives.

Yet there's increasing evidence that having early access to palliative care improves people's mental and emotional health as well as their survival time—with or without access to curative treatments.

In 2007 researchers at the National Hospice and Palliative Care Organization in Virginia, USA, published a groundbreaking study revealing that hospice-based palliative care improves average survival time compared to curative medicine.

Stephen Connor and his colleagues reported that average

survival among terminally ill patients was 29 days longer in palliative care hospice patients compared to non-hospice patients who received curative care in hospital.[12]

His team made this finding by analysing the survival of nearly 4500 patients in six disease groups from a Medicare beneficiary population. The study was a respective cohort study, not a randomised control group design. This means the researchers looked back in time by analysing medical and death records of patients who had died of their disease after choosing one of two options—palliation or curative medicine.

One group of individuals chose a full array of curative medical care while the other group chose hospice-based palliative care aimed at relieving their symptoms and optimising their quality of life, rather than curing their disease.

Average survival was significantly longer in palliative care patients with congestive heart failure, lung cancer and pancreatic cancer, and marginally significant for colon cancer.

On average, palliative patients with pancreatic cancer gained an extra three weeks, those with lung cancer an extra six weeks, and those with congestive heart failure an extra three months of life. There was no difference in average survival between the palliative care group and the curative care group who had either breast or prostate cancer.

The irony here is that less is more. People who accepted their likely prognosis and who chose palliative care in a hospice instead of curative treatment lived longer than those who pursued life-extending therapies.

Three years later, researchers at Massachusetts General Hospital in Boston, USA, made another finding that affirmed the power of palliative care to boost survival time in terminal patients.

Jennifer Temel and her colleagues randomly assigned patients with newly diagnosed metastatic lung cancer to a regimen of either early palliative care integrated with curative oncology care, or oncology care alone.

Patients who had palliation and oncology treatment could also discuss their goals and priorities if their prognosis worsened.

The result? Patients who had palliative and oncology care lived 25 per cent longer (two months) than those who had oncology care alone. They also stopped chemotherapy sooner, entered hospice earlier and experienced better mood and higher quality of life before they died.[13]

What's also interesting is that significantly more palliative patients had their resuscitation preferences noted in their medical records than those who had standard oncology care.

Many experts recommend this as a wise choice. People who record their resuscitation preferences provide clarity about their end-of-life wishes. Doing this can spare our next of kin the burden of making life-prolonging or life-ending decisions in the fog and confusion that can accompany a loved one's final days and moments.

So, how to explain the findings? Jennifer Temel and her team have suggested that the better mood and life quality among patients who had early access to palliative care might have extended their lives.

They've also ventured that better life quality aided the administration of anti-cancer therapy and that early access to palliative care might have contributed to better management of patients' symptoms.

It should be said that these findings aren't conclusive, and anyone faced with end-of-life healthcare choices should discuss their options with their health carers, confidantes and family. But they are part of a growing body of evidence suggesting that early access to palliative care might improve people's mental and emotional health, as well as their survival time—with or without access to curative treatments.

Surviving the odds

How long do people live after they get cancer? It's a useful question, especially when one in two of us will develop a form of cancer in our lifetime.

The answer depends on a host of factors, including the type of cancer, its location and stage of advancement, whether it has spread to other parts of the body, one's age and health at diagnosis, doctors' skills, and the nature and extent of medical treatment.

Cancer survival rates describe the percentage of people who survive a certain type of cancer within a defined time period. Cancer statistics often use a five-year or ten-year survival rate.

In Australia, for example, the five-year survival rate for bladder cancer is 56 per cent, meaning that of all people diagnosed with this cancer, on average 56 in every 100 people are alive five years after diagnosis. By contrast, pancreatic cancer is highly deadly. On average, only eight people in 100 survive five years from diagnosis.[14]

In 1985, the paleontologist Stephen Jay Gould wrote a provocative essay called 'The Median Isn't the Message' after he was diagnosed with abdominal mesothelioma, a rare and deadly cancer, which at that time had an average life expectancy of just eight months.

When he studied the survival curve for his cancer, Gould noticed a lot of variation around the median or midpoint. Although average survival was eight months, many patients survived for shorter and longer time periods. He also noted that the survival curve was skewed to the right with a long tail. This told him that a few rare patients had survived for many years, far longer than the average patient.

Gould decided that he wanted to be among the long-term survivors and he chose a course of treatment involving surgery and chemotherapy, despite the odds that he had only a few months to live.

In his essay, he wrote: 'It has become, in my view, a bit too trendy to regard acceptance of death as something tantamount to intrinsic dignity. Of course, I agree with the preacher of Ecclesiastes that there is a time to love and a time to die—and when my skein runs out I hope to face the end calmly and in my own way. For most situations, however, I prefer the more martial view that death is the ultimate enemy—and I find nothing reproachable in those who rage mightily against the dying of the light.'[15]

Gould was rare and fortunate. He survived another 20 years before dying in 2002 of an unrelated cancer.

But the patients with metastatic lung cancer in Jennifer Temel's study weren't so lucky—even the longest-surviving patients lived little more than three years from their time of diagnosis.

The fact is that some ailments are incurable and highly fatal, regardless of a person's will to live or employ the power of modern medicine. These ailments include conditions like motor neuron disease, the dementias, Parkinson's disease, chronic kidney disease, emphysema, cystic fibrosis, and many of the cancers.

Many who face a more certain and imminent death want a cure. And thanks to human ingenuity, we have the skills, drugs and medical infrastructure for those who want to roll the dice for another shot at life.

Depending on the specifics of a disease and all the other factors affecting survival, some people who choose curative treatments live for many years with deadly conditions, but they often do so with a diminished quality of life and compromised independence. I understand this sentiment because I'm one of them—and I discuss its intimate consequences in chapter six on the subject of uncertainty.

As we've seen, some diseases have a better prognosis than others and can be treated with a high degree of success. But when a prognosis is unpromising—either because the disease is advanced or highly virulent, or it hasn't abated despite several lines of therapy—health professionals may feel pressure to offer more treatments despite their low odds of success.

Palliative care expert Professor Kate White says this about treatment: 'Often when someone is told that their disease isn't responding to treatment, the next question will be, "Well, what else can you offer me?" And I think this puts a clinician in a difficult position because they may respond to the patient by saying, "Well, we could do A or we could just wait and see."

'But the minute something is on the table, it's human nature to choose the A. Now the thing about the A is that if you're sitting on the patient's side, you think, "Well, the doctor wouldn't have mentioned it if they didn't think it was warranted in my case". But on the doctor's side, they may be privately thinking: "Look there is this option, I don't think it's got much of a chance so I'd recommend we take a wait and see approach".'[16]

Testing new therapies

Sometimes the pressure to try new or unproven therapies comes from the medical and pharmaceutical establishments, not the patient. These drugs and therapies come to market because millions of people have been willing to participate in medical trials testing new treatments.

These trials proceed in several 'phases' to ensure the drug or medical device does no harm and has proven efficacy.

Briefly, phase one trials assess how a drug is metabolised, excreted and tolerated, and whether it has any toxic effects on human health.

Perhaps the best illustration of why we need phase one clinical trials is the example of thalidomide—a 1950s drug prescribed for nausea during pregnancy—which caused more than 10,000 birth defects worldwide. Thalidomide wrought havoc because testing for ill effects of the drug weren't detected when it was released to the market.

Phase two trials gather preliminary information about the efficacy of a device or drug based on testing in a small group of people.

Phase three trials, which are usually randomised control trials, often need up to 3,000 or more patients to compare a new drug or device with the current best available therapy or standard of care.

These trials are done to gather evidence about the effectiveness and safety of interventions and they're essential in drug company applications to regulatory authorities like the US Food and Drug Administration before drugs can come to market.

But better drugs and therapies have been bought with the lives and suffering of millions.

The best available evidence reveals that new treatments tested in phase three randomised control trials improve patients' outcomes barely more than 50 per cent of the time compared to existing treatments, and few are substantially better.[17][18]

The finding that patients who receive new treatments do little better than those on existing therapies includes data on both morbidity and mortality outcomes. That is, whether we look at results measuring quality of life or the survival of sick or terminally ill patients assigned to new treatments tested in clinical trials, the results are barely better than established therapies.

What's more, this conclusion is based on the *average* result from the analysis of 860 published and unpublished phase three randomised control trials performed by academics and pharmaceutical companies over the past 50 years.

The results of any particular randomised control trial are impossible to predict. In fact, the ethical underpinning of these trials is that they should be done only when there are genuine uncertainties about the relative merits of alternative treatments.

Therefore, sick or terminally ill people who are offered the opportunity to try a new treatment as part of a clinical trial have no way of knowing their fate. And their chances of seeing an improvement in how they feel or of living longer are actually far less than 50 per cent.

Why? Because the finding that phase three medical trials improve patients' outcomes in barely more than 50 per cent of cases is based on the average result of many hundreds of trials.

For example, while five decades of controlled experimentation has seen cure rates for childhood leukemia improve from almost zero to more than 80 per cent, only two to five per cent of any individual trial of a new treatment provides a real life-saving breakthrough.[19]

Which means this: if you, a loved one or a friend think you want to join a clinical trial of a 'hopeful' new wonder drug, think again.

Doing so is really a gift to future generations. There's little upside for the individual and possibly a lot of downside—the biggest of which are side effects and the impact of false hope.

False hope says hey, thanks for all you did. Thanks for putting your body on the line. We appreciate you making the long trips to the clinic for months on end. And for enduring the protracted waiting times. And for filling in the forms and dealing with the waivers and legal fine print. And suffering the side effects of a new drug we are only beginning to understand. But we're sorry to say it didn't work. You're still sick, you're still terminal, and your precious time is running out.

Uncertainty

> *Our willingness to wonder is where mystery goes for shelter from the steady attack it endures from our demand for information, clarity, and certainty, and from our rarely questioned right to know what we demand to know. Wonder serves mystery with grace and a humble approach. Resolving mystery is like dissecting someone you love to find out how they got so loveable. You might know something you didn't know before, but what you loved gets lost in the inquisition.*
>
> Stephen Jenkinson – *Die Wise: A Manifesto for Sanity and Soul* [20]

Since the Age of Enlightenment and the scientific revolutions that began in the 1500s, Western culture has prized rationality. In matters of philosophy, logic, science, medicine, politics and economics, rational thought and action have transformed every aspect of modern life.

Rationality and ethics have brought democracy, the industrial and technical revolutions, globalised market economics, higher productivity, better living standards and longer lifespans.

But there's a lot about life that won't surrender its secrets, despite our cleverness. Our minds dislike uncertainty and we have a kind of mania for resolving unknowns. But some mysteries call for an approach that's in sympathy with the mythic dimensions of life.[21]

The hidden folds of mystery came to my door five years ago when I was diagnosed with multiple myeloma. Myeloma is a bone marrow cancer affecting the plasma cells, which are a type of white blood cell that make antibodies and fight infection.

Nobody knows what causes it. Epidemiologists have a hunch that something in the environment could play a role, maybe a toxin, a carcinogen or maybe exposure to ionising radiation.

While myeloma's cause is a mystery, my diagnosis did solve one puzzle. For six months prior, I'd endured crippling pain in the ribs, spine and skull and despite rounds of x-rays, blood tests and physical examinations, nobody could pinpoint a cause.

The pain escalated and so did the painkillers I was given, but they did little to lessen the shocking ache that came with any kind of movement. Finally, after six months we got some clues after more blood tests, a bone biopsy and an MRI scan. The MRI showed my bones were riddled with fractures and lesions where they'd been eaten away.

This explained the pain that made everything an agony: sleeping, walking, sitting, even breathing was excruciating. Using the biopsy and blood samples, a medical team zeroed in on the presence of a protein that is a biomarker or sign of myeloma. The normal value of this biomarker—called the light-chain lambda score—is between five and 25. Mine was 2,500—a result that put the diagnosis beyond doubt.

Cancer means that a cell has mutated and reproduced copies of itself many times over to the point where the mutants crowd out normal cells and interfere with normal body functions. The mutations can happen by chance or as a result of a cancer-inducing exposure, usually a toxin or a carcinogen like asbestos, or the chemicals in cigarettes. In my case the mutant plasma cells were being made in the bone marrow—where all blood cells are made—and they were multiplying and crowding out the normal plasma cells. Unlike the normal plasma cells, the cancerous ones were replicating uncontrollably, which had eventually built pressure inside the bones to the point of fracturing them.

Uncertainty

Left unchecked, the cancer cells would eventually invade and shatter the bones in my skeletal system, resulting in permanent pain and major disability.

There's no cure for myeloma. On average, less than half of people (47 per cent) survive five years from the time of diagnosis. One in three survive ten years.[22] When treatment fails, the cancer usually brings on death through complications like kidney failure or fatal blood clots in the lungs.[23]

A medical team recommended I start treatment on a cocktail of chemotherapy drugs to kill the growing cancer cells. According to the biopsy, the cancer cells accounted for 71 per cent of the plasma cells in my bone marrow. If chemotherapy could slash the figure to 15 per cent or lower, I was told I might be a candidate for a stem cell transplant that could put the cancer into remission.

Seven months later the cancer was down to 15 per cent and I'd qualified for an autologous stem cell transplant, which meant collecting and storing stem cells from my blood and reintroducing them a few days after a short burst of high-dose chemotherapy to eradicate the remaining cancer cells.

Stem cells are simple, undifferentiated cells that can turn into specialised cell types like heart muscle cells, blood cells or nerve cells.

Stem cell therapy is a promising area of medical science that harnesses the potential of stem cells to repair diseased and injured tissues. Stem cell transplants are now a standard treatment for myeloma patients.

I was told I could decline the transplant and simply continue on the chemotherapy drugs with regular monitoring to assess their impact on the cancer.

To help me decide I was told the following:

Ninety-five per cent of autologous stem cell transplants are successful, meaning the procedure goes as planned and the stem cells find their way to the bone marrow where they graft successfully and reboot the body's ability to make new cancer-free blood cells.

Lots of things can go wrong in the procedure. Sometimes the stem cells get damaged in the process of harvesting them from the blood, freezing them in liquid nitrogen, and thawing them before they're reinfused into a transplant patient.

Sometimes the graft, whereby the reinfused stem cells make their way to the bone marrow where they are meant to implant themselves and grow into mature, viable blood cells doesn't work, and patients have to repeat the procedure.

The high-dose chemotherapy posed a small but real risk of causing major or fatal damage to several major organs, as well as infections, infertility and the risk of developing other cancers. And although a successful transplant can make myeloma go into remission for a time, it doesn't cure it, and myeloma eventually returns.

Thirty per cent of patients are in complete remission after an autologous stem cell transplant. This means tests show no sign of cancer although it may be present and simply undetectable. The bulk of patients are in partial remission after a transplant, meaning the cancer is still present but at a more manageable level that reduces the odds of the medical risks associated with myeloma, like blood clots and kidney problems. One to two per cent of patients die from the procedure, so that was something to consider too.

Compared to patients who simply take chemotherapy for myeloma, those who take high-dose chemotherapy combined with an autologous stem cell transplant have higher rates of remission, longer periods of remission and longer lives overall.

Finally, patients who have transplants followed by treatment with drugs like thalidomide and bortezomib, when myeloma finally re-emerges, do better than all other patients—including those who don't have transplants.

My choice was clear but there was a world of uncertainty about the risks and benefits embedded in these possible treatment pathways.

For example, a short course of high-dose chemotherapy and a transplant might fail, cause major organ damage, induce other cancers and kill me. Each of these outcomes were small but known risks. This choice also held a 30 per cent chance of remission and a longer life, compared to the option of declining the transplant and simply continuing with long-term chemotherapy.

So, we rolled the dice and I chose the transplant. With my healthy stem cells on ice, I was hospitalised and put on high-dose Melphalan, the chemo drug that would go to work on the residual cancer cells. High-dose chemotherapy is like a sledgehammer. It's a big heavy weapon that kills all rapidly dividing cells, including the body's ability to make new blood cells.

The Melphalan made me weak and extremely ill. Within a week, I had no capacity to make new blood cells and my blood cell counts went to zero. Then came nausea, vomiting, loss of appetite, diarrhoea and insomnia. If I did manage to sleep, I was woken every two hours by a nurse who needed to record my vital signs, take a blood sample and give me drugs to avert infections that could take hold in my weakened state. Then I was reinfused with my healthy stem cells.

I flatlined for several more days before my blood cell counts started to creep back from zero. Fifteen days later, I was weak and bald, but well enough to go home. The stem cell transplant had gone as planned and grafted successfully into my bone marrow where the healthy stem cells had rebooted the blood-cell-making process.

People in remission live in an ambiguous state. Their test results suggest they're free of disease, but there's no way of knowing whether testing has simply failed to detect their disorder.

Now, after five years of chemotherapy, countless biopsies, hundreds of blood tests and a stem cell transplant, the pain's gone, the fractured bones have healed, but the cancer remains.

Four different chemotherapy drugs have failed to eradicate cancer from my body and stopping treatment, even briefly, has seen the cancer surge and spread again.

Not great, but manageable—maybe.

*

Earlier, I remarked that many people who face the prospect of imminent death want a cure. And thanks to modern medicine, some of us get a second shot at life.

That is, some of us get a few more years than similar people from earlier generations, but sometimes this comes with a lower life quality and less independence.

I'm not wedded to living longer at any cost. And like me, I guess most people in treatment for deadly diseases calibrate the tradeoffs between their quality of life and the promise of more time.

Presently, I am tethered to a treatment regimen that means regular hospital visits for infusions of chemotherapy, weekly blood tests and monthly appointments with my doctor.

I get 12 days of freedom between these cycles of chemo, blood tests and medical consultations. In that short window, my body starts to recover from the drugs, and my energy and sleep and mood patterns get a chance to come back to normal.

It also means a free calendar since I've recently stopped

working to focus on other priorities. In those 12 days, I don't have to be anywhere, and if I want, I can take short vacations for excursions or to visit friends for a few days. Long haul vacations to faraway places and friends aren't possible. For now at least, walking Spain's Camino de Santiago trail is off the agenda.

All this is a tiny price to pay for my health and the benefits it allows. So, the question of whether to stay the course, take my medicine and live longer isn't a question. But this isn't true for everyone, as I've said elsewhere.

For some—people ravaged by disease, those suffering the unbearable effects of surgeries and treatments, and those weighing last-ditch therapies that offer almost no chance of beating aggressive or terminal diseases—the scales begin to tip.

If I had doubts about my fortune in having access to great medical care and treatments that gave me a life worth living, I got a reminder at the end of 2017.

After three years in treatment, I was suddenly denied access to drugs that were keeping me alive and well.

At that time, I was able to work full time and pursue a life barely interrupted by treatment and cancer. I was having chemotherapy injections several times a fortnight followed by rest periods.

There were few side effects from the drug (bortezomib) and it was chipping away at the cancer, which had been trending downwards since I'd begun taking it at the start of the year. Bortezomib was my third chemotherapy drug and it had slashed myeloma by 55 per cent.

Although I'd had a lot of fatigue and felt tingling in my toes, indicating possible nerve damage from the drug, bortezomib was better than the two drugs I'd taken since the stem cell transplant. These drugs had initially halted the cancer, but eventually failed to keep it contained.

I had free access to the bortezomib and other chemo drugs because they were listed on Australia's Pharmaceutical Benefits Scheme (PBS). But now, I was going to be denied further access to bortezomib and all other PBS-listed chemotherapy drugs because it hadn't cured the myeloma after 11 cycles of treatment.

This was the very fine print that my doctor and I weren't aware of until access was suddenly shut down.

My doctor wrote to the Federal Department of Human Services appealing the decision to withhold access to PBS-listed chemotherapy drugs. He detailed my medical history and explained that bortezomib was continuing to get results where previous drugs had failed.

Human Services replied with a token rebuff: 'The Department of Human Services does not have any delegation to alter the restriction for this drug, which has been approved by the Pharmaceutical Benefits Advisory Committee for approval as a PBS benefit and it is mandatory that all patients, who are approved by the PBS subsidy of this drug, meet all aspects of the restriction.'[24]

I was stunned. My doctor was angered. My friends and family were outraged. My doctor explained that without ongoing chemotherapy, the cancer would probably surge with unknown and maybe uncontrollable results.

I wrote to the Pharmaceutical Benefits Advisory Committee, a body of experts that assesses and recommends chemotherapy drugs for listing on the PBS, hoping that a human appeal might help.

Dr John Paul, the Secretary of the Pharmaceutical Benefits Advisory Committee replied, saying he was sorry to hear of my diagnosis and the difficulties I faced in getting further treatment but, 'under legislation passed by the Australian Parliament there

Uncertainty

is no provision for the subsidised supply of PBS-listed medicine outside the terms of the PBS listing.'[25]

He cited further rules, regulations and restrictions that meant his hands were bound by red tape and that he couldn't make exceptions.

'There is no provision for exceptions,' he said, 'for individual patients, even in particular cases where the medicine might be beneficial or recommended on clinical grounds.'[26]

In other words, even though bortezomib had succeeded in arresting myeloma and had put it into reverse, and that my doctor was recommending—in fact, pleading—that I be allowed to stay on it, the answer was no, full stop.

However, the medical bureaucrats in Canberra said there was one qualification, one way I might regain access to bortezomib, or perhaps another suitable drug.

The Department of Human Services explained it like this: 'The patient has received 11 cycles of PBS-subsidised bortezomib which is the maximum that is able to be approved under the progressive diseases criteria. A response has been shown so the patient could be entitled to re-treatment if disease progression occurs.'[27]

This meant Human Services was going to deny me a drug that it acknowledged was working, and given this success, I could regain access if, as seemed likely, the cancer spiked again as a consequence of being forced off the drug. Human Services defined 'disease progression' as a 50 per cent increase in the level of cancer. So, the deal was no more chemo, and if myeloma surged in the absence of treatment, my doctor could re-apply for me to re-start bortezomib or another suitable chemo drug.

Taking counsel from my doctor, friends and family, I took leave for three months. I felt I needed to prepare for what lay ahead. If the cancer took off, I wanted to be ready.

As we feared, the cancer started to climb and then rocketed in the absence of chemotherapy. My bones began to fracture and become painful again, and I was back on heavy painkillers.

Loved ones rallied to support me, and the city's broadsheet, *The Sydney Morning Herald*, covered the story to reveal how medical bureaucrats had put my health at risk to preserve their rules—no exceptions.[28]

After four months the cancer biomarker punched through the 50 per cent increase threshold and my doctor and a team of experts agreed that we should try another drug—one that didn't have such draconian restrictions.

Thankfully, the new drug (carfilzomib) went right to work. Almost immediately it smashed the cancer back to a manageable level, my symptoms abated, and I was able to return to work.

*

From a soul perspective, the episode was a reminder to live mindfully and well—to be grateful for the many people who were supporting me, while knowing all the while that death was my muse, my closest companion.

Life is endless, always morphing and re-emerging from the seeds of last season's bloom. There's no closure, no resolution, no certainty, and wishing it were otherwise only brought suffering.

From this standpoint, cancer has been an existential gift—a metaphor for how life and death were having their way with me in an infinitely unfolding mystery. I was a mystery. Cancer was a mystery. Life and death were mysteries.

Embracing these mysteries meant leaping into the void. I tumbled into the abyss all over again. Going into freefall is unnerving till you get the hang of it, because the illusion that we control our destinies is the cultural Kool-Aid that saturates a lot of what we think and feel.[29] [30]

For ego, the void of mystery felt like mayhem, a descent that could end badly unless I found a fix, a solution, an answer—no matter how presumptive, baseless or foolish.

But I knew it would be a mistake to look for deep answers in certainty. My soul knew better and was taking me where I needed to go, even if it felt like chaos to my mind's desire for a solid, reliable answer.

Carl Jung was said to have remarked that if he was forced to choose, he would rather be whole than be good. No stranger to mythology and metaphor, he might have been saying that a capacity to live in a deep and abiding way with mystery is wiser than forcing expedient answers onto inconvenient questions.

Which is why I'm persuaded that engaging in the messiness I feel in the face of mystery might just be a midwife to personhood, to elderhood, and the arts of living and dying well.

If we can, we should

'If we can, we should' has become a kind of mantra in modern medicine. Faced with a choice between certain death, long-term chronic ill health and the tantalising prospect of a cure, few of us can resist choosing more treatment. But the experience of too many people who choose new drugs and aggressive medical interventions isn't what they imagined.

As we've seen, there's a good body of evidence to show that terminally ill people who choose more interventions are likely to endure more illness, more complications and less autonomy than those who choose palliative and hospice care.

They're more likely to die in an intensive care ward of a hospital, tethered to tubes and machines, with little privacy or dignity, often in a setting that imposes a relentless routine of disruption. Deep, restorative, uninterrupted sleep is rare, as anyone who has spent time as a patient in a hospital knows.

This isn't what folks imagine for themselves, nor is it what they expect from modern healthcare. Further, it's light years from the enlightened care that can and should be available to dying people and their grieving loved ones.[31][32]

For people with terminal and life-shortening illnesses, the allure of gaining more time through a medical miracle often involves a fantasy of a life barely interrupted by the therapeutic industrial complex. They might imagine that life-extending or curative therapies will involve a benign and temporary change in circumstances. Unfortunately, this is rarely the case.

If we can, we should

Too often, the side effects of surgery, radiotherapy and other aggressive interventions diminish a person's ability to resume their former life, to say nothing of fulfilling their hopes for a better, longer life.

For five years, Stephen Jenkinson was program director of a palliative care outreach program at a major teaching hospital in Canada. In that role, he witnessed the often-devastating impacts that last-gasp medical interventions had on terminally ill people.

He also saw people who were wholly unprepared for the existential crisis triggered by living longer in the face of a delayed death.

'More time, when it finally kicks in, is the rest of a dying person's life, and the rest of that life will be lived in the never-before-known shadow of the inevitability of their dying. For the first time in their lives they will live knowing that they will die from what afflicts them. More time means more time to live their dying.

'It means more symptoms, more drugs for the symptoms, more drugs for the side effects of the first drugs, more weakness and diminishment and dependence to go along with more time with the kids or grandkids or walks in the park with the dog.

'That's not all it means, not necessarily, but more time almost always means more dying. No one is born, no one walks in the park or sits looking out the window knowing how to die like that, slowly and visibly and knowingly. Very few here on these shores, where death phobia rules, learn how, or want to.'[33]

A lot of simple things can be done to ease the pain and discomfort experienced by sick and dying people. Palliative care doctor BJ Miller has spoken of how little things can make a world of difference in end-of-life care.

One of Dr Miller's patients, Janette, found it harder to breathe due to advancing motor neurone disease. But she decided she wanted to smoke again, not out of a self-destructive bent, but simply to feel her lungs filled while she could still use them.

Kate, another patient, wanted to know her dog Austin was lying at the foot of her bed, to feel his cold muzzle against her dry skin, instead of more chemotherapy coursing through her veins.

Sensuous, aesthetic gratification where we are rewarded for just being is vital, says Dr Miller: 'So much of it comes down to loving our time by way of the senses, by way of the body—the very thing doing the living and the dying.'[34]

Sometimes even palliative care patients require major surgery or radiotherapy to lessen the devastation being wrought, for example, by a metastasising cancer as it strangles and crushes vital organs and viscera in its path.

But every procedure, every incision, every dose of drugs and radiation has an unintended consequence for a person already weakened by their disease and what's done to them in the name of therapeutic healthcare.

So when the time comes, people have a host of different reasons for ending life-extending treatments. Some are philosophical, some spiritual, some financial—and some come down to a conviction that, whatever they might gain in terms of more time, more life isn't worth the cost anymore.[35]

The writer and surgeon, Atul Gawande, has noticed these end-game decisions many times and says people with serious diseases often have higher priorities than prolonging their lives. But not always. Sometimes, people in these circumstances find themselves agreeing to new and even aggressive procedures even though, deep down, they have quite different goals and desires for themselves. Sometimes, the mantra that says 'if we can, we should' is too damned seductive.

Gawande points out that 'surveys find that their (patients') top concerns include avoiding suffering, strengthening relationships with family and friends, being mentally aware, not being a burden on others, and achieving a sense that their life is complete.'

Yet at the same time, he notes, 'our system of technological medical care has utterly failed to meet our needs, and the cost of this failure is measured in far more than dollars.'[36]

Dr Linda Sheahan is a palliative care doctor who consults to health professionals about issues that come to the fore as people approach dying and death. As a palliative care specialist, she's also responsible for the medical needs of dying people.

Dying, and dying well, is more than just a physical experience, she argues.

'Dying well is really no different from living well insofar as it calls for conscious awareness, reflection, planning, and being mindful and good hearted about how we conduct our relationships.

'Dying well is like an action phrase,' she says. 'People die well as part of how they live their life. It's part of the journey, so thinking about it as something separate to life is a category mistake. To the question what does dying well mean, I'd say it means the same thing as living well and ageing well.

'Of course, there are some extra features to mention. From a medical viewpoint, it includes good pain and symptom control. It also calls for good preparation for death—being aware that it's coming and getting ready for dying, and clear decision-making as people approach dying that is informed by clear goals and priorities.

'There are also important existential issues to consider. One is to achieve a sense of completion, meaning that life has fulfilled its meaning. Another is to consider what our legacy is going to be and to complete a life review as part of achieving completion and what we leave behind.

'Achieving completion has several important community dimensions to it, including the gathering together of friends, communion with loved ones, and the resolution of interpersonal conflict. There's also something to consider in terms of reciprocity and our capacity to give something back—to carers, family and loved ones.

'I also think that having an absence of fear helps us to die well—that some sort of peace has been come to—that dying is here—and that it's part of living, and that it's okay. I think this is one of our biggest problems, not just in the medical milieu but in society more broadly. Seeing that our time for dying has arrived can help us to frame the time that is left.'[37]

But with so much cultural impetus driving us to seek cures and the allure of more time, who can guide us on the road less travelled? Who will support us in saying enough is enough? And who can mentor us in our preparations for dying and death?

Youth and ageing

Several years ago the Dalai Lama said it was time to review and complete his preparations for death. This is a subversive view in a time when many of us are preoccupied with youthfulness, and are fearful of ageing and death.[38]

Few of us want to admit our age in a Botox culture where it's a compliment to be told we look youthful, and where surveys of ageing workers reveal that many feel anxious about losing their job or being unable to compete with younger, less wrinkled colleagues.[39]

This might be a clue as to why it's difficult to have conversations that acknowledge and welcome ageing and advancing frailty as inescapable facts of life.

Ageing is often seen as 'less than' rather than a positive accretion of experiences and memories that might be a staging ground for the earned wisdom of elderhood, if only we could stop our fixation on being forever young and disowning the diminishment that comes with advancing years.

From Hollywood to entertainment to mass media, the stories and images and products that sell are brought to us through the lens of youthful perfection.

And even though business and politics are run by white, wealthy, 60-something men, the expanding numbers of older people in the West are nearly invisible in the age of YouTube, unless we're being sold retirement accommodation or incontinence pads.

Ageing people remind us that if we live a full lifespan, we will trace an arc from youth through middle age to old age before we're gathered into our decline and death.

Like a beloved old car, older people show us the wear and tear that's inevitable in the making of a long life journey. Thomas Jefferson, the third US president, once lamented this inevitability to his ageing predecessor, John Adams: '... but our machines have now been running for 70 or 80 years, and we must expect that, worn as they are, here a pivot, there a wheel, now a pinion, next a spring, will be giving way: and however we may tinker them up for a while, all will at length surcease motion.'[40]

Given time, our hair, skin, muscles and bones will grey and weaken, revealing the telltale signs of our advancing years and the ailments that are part of ageing, like arthritis and failing eyesight and diminished hearing.

Meanwhile, the cosmetic surgery market makes an enemy of ageing. In 2015, the global annual market for cosmetic services was put at more than $20 billion, a number set to rise to $27 billion by 2019.[41]

North America accounts for nearly half the global market while growth is also accelerating in Asia, especially among China's growing middle classes.

Facial reconstruction and cosmetic implants top the list of procedures, followed by body contouring procedures involving the reduction and removal of fat, cellulite, skin and veins.

Good business for investors, no doubt, given the global demographics of ageing and humanity's desire to fend off the signs of growing older for as long as possible. Add to that the fact that in concert with environmental factors, some 7,000 genes participate in the ageing process, and we are fighting an unwinnable war.[42] Senescence is programmed into our biology.

Further, our bodies and their constituent cells are constantly bombarded by hazards in the environment. Hazards such as radiation, toxins, viruses and bacteria cause damage that contribute to the dysfunction that characterise the ageing body.

The iconic example of genetic damage as a cause of accelerated ageing is progeria and its related syndromes that are caused by a deficit in the mechanisms involved in DNA repair. The fatal syndrome, which begins in early life, causes rapid ageing and deterioration. Children with progeria die from heart disease and have an average life expectancy of 14 years.

Prematurely aged and destined to die by their mid-teens, these children are a lightning rod for fundraising and research, and have provoked books, movies and TEDx Talks aimed at raising awareness and finding a cure. But science has a long way to go before it can stay the forces of ageing, whether it is applied to the pathologies of accelerated ageing such as progeria or to the 'natural' changes that accompany senectitude and its sequalae.

For now, at least, senescence and death are encoded in our DNA. They are like cousins, once removed, just as the Greeks saw sleep (hypnos) and death (thanatos) as twins.[43] From DNA's viewpoint, your genetically determined purpose is to pass on its code and die, so life can feed on you to propagate and continue. This is your programmed mission, no other.

Even so, today's smart money, which is being invested by 30- and 40-somethings, is a bet on eternity, a cancer-free life lived on Mars.[44][45] So, we live and dream of immortality. Like the dysfunctional family from the American sitcom *Arrested Development*, as a culture we are pursuing extravagant decadence in the face of our changed and changing circumstances. The financially ruined Bluth family in *Arrested Development* want to eat, drink and spend like there's no tomorrow. No limits and no consequence to their debauchery and intemperance. But they still want to show up tomorrow and do it all over again.

Can we stay young and grow wise? Can we claim life and be ageless? Can we have our cake and eat it too?

These questions misconceive the nature of life and death. In many of the myths, the god of death is also the god of life because the cultures that spawned these myths understood that the two are one and the same.[46] In Haitian voodoo culture, Ghede is the god of death and fertility. In ancient Egyptian mythology, Osiris is the god of the afterlife and the generator of life.

Life and death appear as opposites because of temporality—the linear progression of past, present and future. From a personal standpoint, we are born, we live and we die, but from a universal stance, life and death are mechanisms that are endlessly recycling energy and genetic material. The same is true on a cosmic scale. The endless birth and death of stars reveal this same unity, the oneness of all things.

The mythic hero who sacrifices his or her life for another knows there's no birth without death. The Christ who died to the flesh is reborn in the spirit. Each generation must die and give way to the next. So, death ensures that life continues even though our little ego selves do not continue. As soon as we create a life we become the walking dead. Our only task is to protect and nurture new life. And if we live a long life? There are no formulas, but in time we might be tempered by our decline and life's calamities into becoming elders.

Meanwhile, time is marking itself on our ageing bodies with the beauty of an artist who might be saying: *the wheel of life has turned a thousand times, but your time isn't done. Your hard-won lessons are needed, so stay a while longer. And so, here, and here, and here, I mark your body-vessel with the signs of ageing so that others will see your submission, your regression and your magnificence.*

The tyranny of hope

Hope is a desire or expectation for something to happen—usually something we place a high value on.

Some health professionals say fostering hope should always be a part of the conversation when they speak to a terminally ill person about their prognosis and end-of-life care.

This is natural and understandable, but it's worth noting that this notion is rooted in a belief that hope is always positive—an inherently virtuous and essential mindset for creating a rosy and optimistic future for ourselves.

According to some palliative care and cancer-nursing textbooks, hope can also improve a patient's symptoms, immune function, mental health and quality of life.[47][48]

As an example, here's an excerpt from a peer-reviewed academic journal on medical ethics that typifies this thinking.

'Hope, with its in-built orientation towards the future, is a centrally important part of every person's life. Without hope, we can hardly form intentions to act, or see reasons to do so. To take away a person's hope is to consign that person to despair and its concomitant paralysis of action.

'Sustaining hope in the patient, therefore, is an important element in all healthcare. But how are we to think about hope in the context of palliative care, where we are dealing with people who are terminally ill, and who know themselves to be so?

'Here as elsewhere, the welfare and quality of life of a patient is likely to be substantially better if she can maintain an attitude of hope towards achieving positive goals. And if we take seriously the dictum, widely endorsed throughout palliative care, that "patients should live until they die", then supporting the patient's hope may seem to be an important part of the palliative carer's activities.'[49]

Two decades ago, University of Chicago scholars Nicholas Christakis and Elizabeth Lamont investigated prognostic error among doctors.[50]

What they learned was unnerving and astounding.

They found that doctors' prognoses were accurate only 20 per cent of the time. Also, nearly two-thirds of doctors' predictions about patients' survival were overestimates (63 per cent), and overall, doctors overestimated patient survival by a factor of five. Not surprisingly, the tendency for doctors to make prognostic errors was lower among more experienced doctors.

But what surprised many was that the better that doctors knew their patients—which was measured by the length and recentness of their contact—the more likely they were to make mistakes.

Not only did the length of doctor-patient relationships predict more prognostic errors, but most doctors were overly optimistic.

Meaning that doctors who had a close and long-standing association with terminally ill patients were more likely to wrongly believe that their patients had longer to live than they did.

Christakis and Lamont say the findings could have ominous repercussions.

First, a doctor's undue optimism about a patient's survival prospects might mean she doesn't refer a patient early enough to palliative care, a decision that could negatively affect a patient's quality of life.

Said another way, the failure by two out of three doctors to predict how little remaining time a patient has left could mean they fail to make an appropriate referral to life-preserving medical care or palliation.

Second, the failure by many doctors to predict and communicate accurate prognostic information could mean patients make poor treatment choices.

It's been shown, for example, that terminally ill cancer patients who have overly optimistic beliefs about their survival tend to choose aggressive procedures that have major side effects, in preference to non-aggressive palliative care where the goal is to maintain or improve quality of life.[51]

But why would a longer doctor-patient relationship affect a doctor's prognostication? And why do so many make errors on the upside by telling patients they have more time than they do?

Author Stephen Jenkinson wonders whether a long-term doctor-patient relationship binds a doctor to her patient's hopes, thereby compromising her medical judgment, despite evidence to the contrary. Or maybe something subtler is at work.

He says, 'It is not the content of what is wished for—the grail of More Time—that is contagious. The fact that the patient steadfastly wants what is already gone for good, often long after it is gone; perhaps this is the contagious thing.

'The patient's insatiable desire for what will never be makes the doctor's simple objectivity and prognosis look and feel ineffectual and impotent, even disloyal. Many a physician has been accused of giving up on patients when they attempt to refer those patients to palliative care. It looks as though sympathy and discernment are hard bedfellows.'[52]

Whether hope helps terminally ill people is unproven, despite claims that it helps them cope with impending death.

So, if hope is unproductive maybe we should ask, what if it's harmful?

The tyranny of hope

A more pointed question is this: what happens when a terminally ill person's hopes for a cure, or remission, or more time, is finally obliterated in the face of looming death?

By definition, hopeful dying people are never where they want to be—their present state is intolerable because they're hoping for a better future that might come to pass, but probably won't. They have what they don't want and want what they haven't, which is a prescription for a world of suffering.[53]

One of Buddhism's central insights is that resisting reality creates mental and emotional suffering.[54][55] Resistance is opposition to something, be it a thought, feeling, sensation, perception or action. It arises from a judgment that the status quo is unacceptable and that something should be done to change it.

Eckhart Tolle has said that the mental and emotional anguish we feel is proportional to our level of resistance to reality.[56] Resistance is a refusal to acknowledge and accept the status quo—a denial of the way things are. This resistance is always counterproductive: even the tiniest sliver of non-acceptance or denial produces an equivalent quantum of mental and emotional pain for ourselves.

Tolle argues that when we acknowledge and accept reality, we drop our energetic opposition to the truth and thereby experience less suffering. Furthermore, when we give our full attention to our present life circumstances, rather than the past or future, and unlearn the tendency to judge and label our experiences, we can tap into what he calls 'the power of now'.

There's now good academic evidence from randomised control trials that being 'present' or 'mindful' and dropping habitual mental chatter can be pathways to states of peace, bliss and well-being.[57][58]

These practices—being in the here and now and having a quiet mind—can evoke the same tranquil state as meditation, because they are essentially the same phenomenon. Being aware of what's happening while it's happening is to be present to life unfolding. And letting it be as it is without physical, mental and emotional resistance brings us into accord with life, instead of opposing it.

But hope puts dying people into opposition to their circumstances. It labels the anticipated future as unacceptable or traumatic or frightening, and insists on a hoped-for future where death, illness or suffering should be opposed, or put off for another time.

Dying people aren't alone in this endeavour. Often, they're encouraged to be hopeful by their professional carers and loved ones. In fact, terminally ill people who don't invest in being hopeful risk being told they're depressed or that they have a 'negative attitude'.

Finally, the time comes when reality is undeniable and the consensus finally admits that it's okay for a dying person to die. But too often people in these circumstances have had to wait till they're ravaged by symptoms, or the ill effects of too much medical treatment, before they're allowed to do so.

The great tragedy here is that investing in perpetual hope means dying people may never learn how to die. Even when dying is nearly upon them, they may be reaching for any means, averting what dying requires and demands.

In large part, the skyrocketing demand for antidepressants, terminal sedation and medically assisted suicide are the progeny of our culture's dogged refusal to craft a wisdom from dying. And this is why it's so hard to die at this time in human history—why it's nearly impossible to be 'wrecked on schedule', as Stephen Jenkinson calls it.

The surgeon and author Sherwin Nuland admitted that at

times he pushed back against dying and death by refusing to let his patients die at their appointed time and unintentionally intensified their suffering.

'Death belongs to the dying and to those who love them,' he says. 'Though it may be sullied by the incursive havoc of disease, it must not be permitted to be further disrupted by well-meant exercises in futility. Decisions about continuation of treatment are influenced by the enthusiasm of the doctors who propose them.

'Commonly, the most accomplished of the specialists are also the most convinced and unyielding believers in biomedicine's ability to overcome the challenge presented by a pathological process close to claiming its victim.

'A family grasps at a straw that comes in the form of a statistic; what is offered as objective clinical reality is often the subjectivity of a devout disciple of the philosophy that death is an implacable enemy. To such warriors, even a temporary victory justifies the laying waste of the fields in which a dying man has cultivated his life.

'I say these things not to condemn high-tech doctors. I have been one of them, and I have shared the excitement of last-ditch fights for life and the supreme satisfaction that comes when they are won. But more than a few of my victories have been pyrrhic. The suffering was sometimes not worth the success.'

In pointing the finger at himself, Dr Nuland, who was a surgeon at Yale-New Haven Hospital for three decades, confessed that he had persuaded his brother, Harvey, who was dying of metastatic colon cancer, to try a last-gasp experimental treatment when it had little chance of success.[59] Nuland later confessed that he had mistakenly tried to give his brother hope by making death, not disease, the enemy.

Knowing full well the temptation among doctors to pursue last-ditch cures, he resolved that he'd never allow a physician to play God as he had.

'When I have a major illness requiring highly specialized treatment, I will seek out a doctor skilled in its provision. But I will not expect of him that he understands my values, my expectations for myself and those I love, my spiritual nature, or my philosophy of life. That is not what he is trained for and that is not what he will be good at. It is not what drives those engines of his excellence. For those reasons, I will not allow a specialist to decide when to let go.

'I will choose my own way, or at least make the elements of my own way so clear that the choice, should I be unable, can be made by those who know me best.

'The conditions of my illness may not permit me to "die well" or with any of the dignity we so optimistically seek, but within the limits of my ability to control, I will not die later than I should simply for the senseless reason that a highly skilled technological physician does not understand who I am.'[60]

Annihilation

A living culture provides an affirmative meaning for death through its myths and rituals. But today, in the West at least, death is a feared and loathsome thing because it means annihilation—something TS Eliot put his finger on almost a century ago when he said we no longer have the cultural tools or mythologies to infuse death with meaning.[61]

In a post-religious era, death is a kind of desolation and without a mythological or cultural story to feed or sustain us, we feel obliterated. We imagine dying means vanishing into the void. That all is lost.

As a result, death phobia lies at the heart of our institutions and endeavours, and nowhere is this more apparent than in the training of our health professionals and the services rendered by healthcare.

Our fear of death is like a frenetic engine, driving the development of limitless pills and potions and procedures engineered to deny and delay the inevitable, at great cost to everyone involved.

But resisting death is a denial of nature. If we look out the window into a garden we can see the cycle of life and death everywhere. Life feeds on the death of everything, and death comes to all, whether by accident, design, disease or predation.

But we've conspired against ourselves to live and die outside nature's lore, without tutors or guides to help us navigate a journey none can avoid. So, we have no affinity, or intimacy, or adequate language to bring to our decline and dying.

This is why we come to death and dying as rank amateurs: we're ignorant and alone, and too often afraid. It's why we struggle to tell each other, even long before death comes calling, that we feel broken-hearted by death—by ours and the deaths of those we love.

But the broken-heartedness experienced by the living and the dying isn't the same thing. The secret theology of our rational, secular age is that the dead don't need anything from the living. If people who've died have lived morally then believers in a hereafter say they're qualified to enter their heavenly reward. And if they haven't, then eternal damnation awaits.

For atheists, the dead are simply dead, full stop. Either way, the living cannot and need not intercede on behalf of the dead, nor have a relationship with them. So, we've come to believe death ruptures our capacity for a relationship with the dead because they're gone. They're gone because the past is gone. They're gone because our lives are bounded by duality and our concept of time, which is linear and always moving from the present into an infinite future.[62] [63]

But it's the *consignment* of our dead to a time-bound concept of the past which is the source of their gone-ness. And the consequences cut both ways. Dying people know they're about to disappear from the lives of the living. They know because, like us, they have been able to 'move on' from the deaths of old friends and loved ones by putting them into the gone-ness of the past.

But most of us don't foresee our annihilation when we consider the end of our days. We imagine our worst fears to be uncontrolled pain, losing control, dying alone, and maybe judgment day, or a fear of the unknown.

But what really hits hard for dying people is that soon they'll be forgotten. They learn that the living will mourn for a time and

Annihilation

move on. And if the bereaved have trouble adjusting to grandpa's death, then drugs and sympathy and counselling are readily available.

So, the language of loss has infused the language and meaning of death. The upshot is we imagine the past and the dead are gone. And we grieve because our imaginations have been colonised to believe the dead have vanished.[64]

This is why we carry mementos like photos and trinkets and objects—to remind ourselves of those we call the 'dearly departed'. It's why dying people these days are so fond of making farewell video clips—so we can summon their digital presence from the void of death at funerals and wakes and anniversaries.

In name, these memorial services are about the dead but they're not really for them. They're for *us*, the living, because they're about our mourning, our loss. So, when dying people come to this awareness, they realise there can be no relationship between the living and the dead. They're about to enter the void of the long forgotten—where life and death go separate ways.

According to this mantra, death ends relationships and reciprocity—that is, the mutual responsibility we have to the world and to each other that's rooted in the infinite interdependence of all matter, all phenomena.[65]

But if death ends relationships and reciprocity, it makes for a long and lonely experience for everyone concerned.

However, there are countercultural stories that wonder about the river of time and the past, and what it means to be eternal. Some, like *Die Wise: A Manifesto for Sanity and Soul* wonder whether life flows towards the past and all that came before us.[66] In this story, the dead aren't gone; they're destiny.[67]

This theme recurs in what might be called 'spiritual' art and literature. In Herman Hesse's classic novel, *Siddhartha*—the story of a young man on a spiritual quest during the time of the Buddha—his protagonist comes to see time as an illusion and that all things are unified and connected by the cyclical unity of nature.[68]

In the three-faced *Trimurti* sculpture inspired by Hindu and Buddhist writings, the central face is the mask of eternity that transcends time and duality. By contrast, the second and third faces represent opposites—a reminder that *antitheses* are the product of dualistic thinking in the field of time: good and evil, male and female, past and present.[69]

These narrative and artistic insights regard our ideas of loss as illusion—a consequence of an ideology that obliges us to feel orphaned when the people we love and care for die. But the trance of 'loss' is just that—a kind of daze, camouflaged as something rational and reasonable that consigns the past and the dead to the void of annihilation.

One impact is that if we don't speak of dead people in the past tense soon after they die, people around us start getting worried; they start wondering about our mental health. Another is that annihilating our dead compounds our homelessness—meaning the felt experience of belonging to nothing and no one—a devastating reality known to countless people around the world.

Life and death are mysteries. But *knowable* mysteries. Shakespeare reminded us that life is more than a human thing. It's something we *participate* in. *Life* is the play, he said, and the play's the thing ... we're merely *players*.[70]

Death is knowable too, but understanding it means awakening from ignorance—*remembering* who I truly am so that I can *embody* my true nature.

Our human life is as brief as a 'lightening flash', said the Buddha. What if you came to your dying moment and still didn't

Annihilation

know who you were? The Sufi poet, Rumi, said knowing who we are is the 'one thing' we must do. Do this, and there's 'nothing to worry about,' he said. But forget this, and you'll have 'done nothing in your life.'

A year to live

Stephen Levine sat at the bedside of thousands of dying people for a quarter-century or more. Over that time, he noticed remarkable transformations in many who were living their last days and months.

For some, approaching death was a catalyst for heartfelt changes that made their remaining time exceptional and rewarding. Many turned towards life in a way they hadn't before, and Levine wondered whether some of this renewal could be transplanted into the midst of our lives, before death came knocking.

His enquiry was the genesis for *A Year to Live*, a book that records the experiences and reflections from a time when he and his wife, Ondrea, spent a year living as if it were their last.

A Year to Live is a guide for taking stock and reviewing life with the intention of growing one's capacities for compassion and gratitude and forgiveness, and to bring more focus to living mindfully.[71] To that end, it describes practices to help people explore their thoughts and feelings about their death—and to consider what is deathless.

Part of the genius of taking a year to live as if it were one's last is that healthy people have the luxury of doing so without the challenge and turmoil that accompany dying. Skeptics have said living a year as if it were one's last in the midst of perfect health is a con. Maybe it is.

But Levine and others who've taken the year-long experiment say it creates an impetus for renewal, and that, in the years that followed, many have felt enriched and less limited to their old ways and habits.

Levine's book is more than a guide to cherishing life and making the uncharted journey to death. It is an *aide memoire* for what he calls 'the restoration of the heart which occurs when we confront our life and death with mercy and awareness ... an opportunity to resolve our denial of death as well as our denial of life in a year-long experiment in healing and revitalization.'[72]

Levine asks, what would you do if you knew your days were numbered by the certainty of impending death?

'When we ask ourselves this question, myriad possibilities arise. We spin through the full range of our fantasies—from orgies to monasteries and back again. Even on first reflection it becomes painfully obvious that the psychological momentum of our approaching demise propels a heavy wind before it.

'In this wind tumble the fallen leaves of our abandoned dreams and thwarted melodies. It chills us to the marrow. The question reminds us of how much we have forgotten.

'A part of us begins to panic at the thought that it hasn't had quite enough time to leave something valid behind. There have been so few moments when life was all it was cracked up to be; so much that might have been different had the heart not been obstructed by fear.

'As we begin to see where we have been absent from life, increasing possibilities audition for our approval. The heart suggests that we become more present, that we sharpen our focus. When death, the big wind, blows out our birthday candles, only the wish remains; and only that longing, which deepens our wisdom and compassion.'[73]

Levine offers an antidote to the idea that our last year of life might be spent ticking off the items on our bucket list—meaning our deferred ambitions and pleasures—an idea popularised by the film of the same name.[74] Our remaining time *could* be spent on our bucket list, but that's not *all* it could mean.

I took the year to live experiment seven years ago. The experience both narrowed and expanded my focus and gave me reasons to unpack and process decades of backlog.

I was stunned by what I'd deferred and avoided. I was appalled to learn how much pain I was holding and how much energy I was devoting to avoidance—of decisions, pain, memories and people in my life.

I learned that I was living in denial of death and busting through denial helped me make different choices about what I was giving energy to: who I spent time with; who I'd pushed away; who I wanted to thank; and who and what I wanted to let go of.

A year later I formed a group that did 'a year to live' together. We met each month to share our insights and the changes we were making, and somewhere in the process I realised there was a black hole of truth at the bottom of my fear of life and death.[75]

Getting to the truth meant clearing the debris and distractions to get to the sinkhole at my core. Everything I'd constructed—my character, my desires, my attachments, my preoccupations—were in the way.

Most importantly, I was in the way. Ego was plugging the hole, and when I recognised this I went into freefall. Like young Alice in Lewis Carroll's *Alice in Wonderland*, I went tumbling down the rabbit hole.[76]

Grief

I touched into grief the night my father died. The call came from my stepmother, Yina: 'Frank has had a heart attack. He's dead!'

Like the poet William Stafford hearing the news of his father's death, I drove in from the west that night to find her at the lighted door. Like Stafford, I too stood in the darkness—on the threshold of truth, still a truant from knowing.

There was a story from the past that my father and I had told and retold over the years, of how we parked the car one night in a downpour and walked to the end of a seawall. Like Stafford and his father, we were cut off, out there in the darkness alone.

We stood together, casting our lines. The rain hammered, lashing the foaming sea as a tiny boat, tossed on the whitecaps, sliced the darkness. And like Stafford, we too stood composed, knowing we could go home.

Circle of Breath

The night my father died

the moon shone on the snow.

I drove in from the west;

mother was at the door.

All the light in the room extended

like a shadow. Truant from knowing,

I stood where the great dark fell.

There was a time before, something
we used to tell--how we parked
the car in a storm and walked into
the field to know how it was to be
cut off, out in the dark alone.
My father and I stood together
while the storm went by.

A windmill was there in the field
giving its little cry, while we
stood calm in ourselves, knowing
we could go home.
But I stood on the skull of the world
the night he died, and knew that
I leased a place to live
with my white breath.
Truant no more, I stepped forward
and learned his death.

William Stafford [77]

He'd been laid on an old rug on the floor of his bedroom. Placed there by the police attending the scene who took my name as they passed me a business card and offered condolences.

I knelt in close, head to head, and cradled him. The police withdrew from the doorway, giving us space. He was the same but different. Intensely familiar but the habits of our old intimacy had fled. The wink, the nod, my hand in his big brawny mitt. His gentle squeeze that said, *I love you*. I took his hand by impulse, squeezed and said, *I love you, too, dad* as the tears came, *truant no more*, wetting both our faces.

Death disrupts the habits of a lifetime. My old partner could no longer play his part in our long running double-act. I grieved for both of us. For what we'd shared, for what we hadn't, and for what had ended.

The next day, I went to the morgue to see him again with one of my sisters. We sat with him in a small viewing room, still awed by his presence. Shocked by his new silence. I lingered after my sister vacated the room. I needed to talk to him for a while longer and touch him again for the last time.

I rang John, a mate whose father had recently died. John knew my father and I knew his, and he'd rung me many times as his father lay dying, and later, in the wake of his death.

He picked up and I told him I was sitting with dad, my late father, Frank Gaffney. I shared my shock and my grief. The unexpected suddenness of his passing. How I'd taken him to lunch for his birthday, just a week before. Chinese at the local RSL club where he'd played host, recommending choice dishes while he insisted on buying the beers. A couple of Guinness for the Irishman and his boy, his firstborn.

Like always, we traded news, stories, jokes, gossip. He asked me about my cancer, I asked about his litany of chronic diseases. He was a walking miracle. Nothing could kill him, I thought. I'll die before he does.

And now this, I told John. *The end of an era.*

Desire

The idea of doing a bucket list raises the question of whether it's possible to live a full life without satisfying all of our desires. Do limits mean less?

Human history shows that humans treat the world as a need-gratification machine. We farm its plants and animals to fill our bellies. We mine its minerals and fossil fuels to drive industry. We've turned mountains into slag heaps in the name of jobs and growth and higher living standards. No forest or river or endangered species can stand in the way of profit and progress.

Some of us wring our hands at the desecration of the oceans and skies, but still we plunder and pollute like there's no tomorrow. We tell ourselves we're determined to shrink our footprint for the sake of our grandchildren. We say we're committed to reducing fossil fuel emissions and the carbonisation of the atmosphere that is heating the Earth, but together we are unleashing untold damage to the biosphere and the ecological basis for life.

In 2015, it was calculated that 23,000 of the world's 73,000 known assessed species were threatened with extinction.[78] In 2019, a global assessment reported that 25 per cent of assessed animal and plant groups were threatened, suggesting that about one million species face extinction, many within decades, unless action is taken to reign in the drivers of biodiversity loss.[79]

The combined effects of rising human population, global warming, uncontrolled poaching, invasive species and habitat destruction are accelerating species extinction and shrinking biodiversity at an unprecedented rate.[80] Today, the average extinction rate is between 1,000 to 10,000 times faster than the rate that prevailed over the past 60 million years.[81]

One example. In 2015, the death of one of four remaining northern white rhinos caused headlines around the world. It's a textbook case of our attack on nature and the blindness that shields us from knowing the cost of our actions.

It's also a tale of how we're using medical science to resurrect life from the ashes of destruction when, all the while, we're hell bent on destroying it.

In November that year, media outlets reported the death of Nola, a 41-year-old female rhinoceros in San Diego Zoo Safari Park.[82][83] Zoo veterinarians euthanised Nola, though many reports omitted this detail, preferring to say she died after age-related health issues and a lingering infection 'caught up with her'.

Captured in southern Sudan in 1975, she spent all but the first 18 months of her life in captivity, first at Dvůr Králové Zoo in the Czech Republic and from 1989 at San Diego Zoo, California.

Nola never conceived and now the world's three remaining rhinos (two females, one male) are considered too old to reproduce naturally.

Throughout her captivity, science was used to coax Nola into conceiving in the hope of averting the extinction of her species (*Ceratotherium simum cottoni*) whose numbers crashed from 2,000 to just three in the past 50 years. Population numbers have plunged mainly because of uncontrolled hunting and poaching.

In 1990, Nola was joined at San Diego Zoo by Angalifu, a 20-year-old male rhino. When she 'resisted' his advances, zoo staff dosed her food with prostaglandin and progesterone in a bid to make her more receptive. The two finally mated but she never conceived.

In death Nola has been pressed into service as a science marketing tool for defying the inevitable: species extinction. Scientists performed a post-mortem on her 4,000-pound carcass to remove tissue for use in a range of reproductive possibilities.

In theory, Nola might live on to 'save' her species through applications like artificial insemination, in-vitro fertilisation, embryo transfer, genetic engineering, or by hybridising her remains with a member of the more populous southern white rhino.[84] All this will take decades and millions of dollars with no certainty of success.

To further her contribution to science, Nola's body now resides at the National Museum of Natural History at the Smithsonian Institution as part of its research collection.

Captured, caged, drugged, mated, euthanised, bio-banked and acquired for reproductive research—Nola is a symbol of our inhumanity and our refusal to live in harmony with nature, or to recognise that all this gee-whiz science is putting the cart before the horse.

Today, humans are using the equivalent of 1.5 planets per year to meet their demand for resources and to absorb their toxic waste stream. This means that it takes Earth 18 months to regenerate what we consume and cast aside every year.

Unchecked human consumption is unleashing catastrophic damage on an unprecedented scale and despite the mountain of evidence that we're at a tipping point, we're still living beyond our means, and the laws of nature.

But it wasn't always so.

'Older ways of life know the world as animate, as alive. That means the world is treated with the same regard and esteem as every living thing in it,' writes Stephen Jenkinson.

'People living these older ways of life know themselves as of the world, made of the same things, in the same ways. In modern, sophisticated ways of life the world is inert and inanimate, a staging ground for life, but not alive itself.

'People living in that way tend to feel a bit like visitors or strangers to the world, uniquely wrought. But this faith in the unprecedented, singular self turns out legions of solitary, stand-alone people. This faith is hard on companionship. These people fan out over the countryside, compelled by need, bent on getting those needs met.'[85]

Business as usual is unsustainable but there's no sign that we're about to change an ideology that's driving us all to extinction. But the proposition that we could live and die with unmet needs and desires is intolerable only because we say so.

Stephen Levine has related the story of a man with cancer who wanted to complete his life by 'finding his lotus' before he died. He reveals how the man's relationship to desire was the source of his dissatisfaction and suffering, and that gradually, he saw that it wasn't *having* what he wanted that brought him satisfaction but rather the *absence* of desire.

'He mentioned that when something wanted was received, he noticed a momentary spiking of pleasure and the experience we call satisfaction. But to his surprise the satisfaction didn't come from the having but from the momentary flash of getting when the light of his great nature was no longer obstructed by a mind full of desire.

'It was the absence of desire, which offered the feeling of satisfaction, of temporary completeness. The very nature of desire was one of dissatisfaction with any moment in which the object of desire was not present. This recognition of the painful nature of desire didn't make him desire-less but (it) allowed him to treat desire with a new respect.'[86]

You can chase what you think you want and need. You can live your life pursuing a bucket list. And in conventional terms, achieving these things might look and feel like success and richness. But there are profound consequences for your grandchildren and the planet that will reverberate for eons.

Deeper still, meeting our desires in this way isn't what it seems because it misconceives what we are, what we owe, and what brings us true satisfaction.

Reciprocity

Many of us understand that our way of life is having a destructive impact on the basis for life on Earth. Some of us are moved to do something about it by changing our ways and shrinking our ecological footprints.

We're reducing, recycling and re-using resources. Maybe we're cultivating some home-grown fruit and veggies to reduce the impacts of unsustainable farming. Or we're harvesting solar power and water from our rooftops to reduce carbon emissions and the demand for scarce water.

Individually, these actions are making a small and positive difference. And they're being replicated on a larger scale by mindful corporations and investment funds that support 'clean capitalism'. The emergence of national and international emissions trading schemes are another hopeful sign that we're moving to ways that harmonise with nature and sustainability.

But our collective lives have damaged Earth's ecosphere and biosphere in ways that can't be undone in our lifetime. Maybe many lifetimes. The harm we've done since the dawning of the industrial age is baked-in, and the effects of the way that 7.3 billion people live today will reverberate for decades, if not centuries.[87][88][89]

This trajectory underlines the common sense of living in harmony with nature and the tenets of 'sustainable development'. It also highlights the wisdom of old ways rooted in an understanding of reciprocity, and the attitudes of esteem and gratitude that informed our old hunting and gathering practices.

These old ways taught people that they were made of the same stuff as the world and its inhabitants—namely, earth, wind, fire and water.

During those times, people understood that their way of life—and their true nature as humans—were identical to the plants, the animals and the greater world. Their lore said: *the world needs you, and it's your responsibility to care for the world just as it cares for you and the community.*

Rebecca Adamson, a Cherokee leader and activist spent her summers in the Smoky Mountains with her maternal grandparents, from whom she learned Indian ways and values in Qualla territory—land held in trust for the Eastern Band of Cherokee Indians. Her words illustrate how reciprocity—giving and receiving—is fundamental to the web of life.

> *Let there be no purpose in giving, save reciprocity.*
>
> *For to a people whose spirituality lies within Life's wholeness*
>
> *Who share the gifts of the sky and the mountains and the seas and the forests*
>
> *Who exchange abundance in the circle of animal brethren,*
>
> *Giving is not a matter of pure altruism and benevolence*
>
> *But a mutual responsibility*
>
> *To make the world a better place.*
>
> *Let there be no purpose in receiving, save reciprocity.*
>
> *For a society whose belief in humanity lies within the interdependence of people*
>
> *Who hold to the deeply universal good of community values and*
>
> *Where children are the generation of our People*
>
> *Giving is seen in the entirety of receiving.*
>
> *Let the reciprocity of giving lie in a deepening of the Circle of Life.*

Reciprocity

For as with Life where

The root needs to receive in order for the plant to give fruit

It can be seen that in the honor of giving

As in the honor of receiving

Good is only realized by the contributions of both.[90]

*

Our individual needs often trump the needs of the common good. If an individual can afford to have his needs met, he does, and to hell with the rest of us. But on a global scale, the ecological costs of living this way are catastrophic.

So, changing our ways and living mindfully in our day and age mean taking account of the mounting debt that we're passing to future generations as we try to reign it in—a kind of shell game that means living the lunacy of forever taking more than we can ever repay.

This should spur us to craft a wisdom from the heartbreak of what we're doing—by becoming more responsible for our actions, instead of succumbing to the seduction of being otherwise.

What do we really need? How should we meet our needs? Will we leave the world with a debt or are we willing to change our ways to leave it in a state of abundance?

Stephen Jenkinson has considered these questions deeply: 'This older calculation of need weighs the accumulation of a kind of obligation to the world accrued by those who pursue it, the kind of obligation bequeathed to coming generations.

'When the hole left by trying to meet that need is deeper and wider than people's ability to begin to fill it through their way of living, worshipping and loving, then the balances tip, and the obligation is not something people can deliver on.

'When that unlived debt—perhaps unlivable debt—is about to be passed on to their children's children, then what is being pursued is no longer deemed a need. It is too expensive, and anything that expensive is not in the realm of human need.'[91]

In truth, our needs are small compared to what the world needs from us. Yet we are so indebted that almost nothing we do can make a dent in what we owe.

This needn't mean that all is lost even though some scientists believe global warming and the unravelling of the web of life is irreversible. Moreover, letting ourselves succumb to pessimism would be a moral failure that only hastens catastrophe. We can't allow ourselves the luxuries of despair or inaction. As the Anthropocene doubles down, the only moral response is positive and urgent action.[92]

There's no mystery about how we got to this point. For too long humans have treated the world and its sentient creatures as exploitable resources whose function is to feed, clothe and warm themselves. When this mindset got hitched to the engines of industry and was supercharged by the mantra of limitless growth, no mountain or river or threatened species could stand in the way.

Modern economies have never been so indebted. Their income and productivity are dwarfed by their borrowings and the interest on what they owe. When the global financial crisis of 2009 destroyed wealth on an unprecedented scale, governments responded by employing the magic pudding of quantitative easing—'printing money' backed by more debt in the form of treasury bonds and mortgage-backed securities.

These bonds are a promise to repay capital with interest years down the track. It's a kind of junkie wisdom that means debt-addicted economies can defer debt payments into the never-

never. Quantitative easing employed by the US Federal Reserve between 2008 and 2014 was the largest economic stimulus program in history, doubling debt on the Fed's balance sheet from US$2.106 trillion to US$4.486 trillion.

This refusal to accept limits—financial and ecological—echo our own denial of human limits. Our obsession with everlasting youthfulness, our disavowal of ageing and our fear of death are bedfellows to the pursuit of ever-rising living standards and debt-based growth. They are symptoms of the same *dis-ease*. Signs of the same selfish willfulness writ large on the world.

We pursue personal pleasure, fulfilment and self-aggrandisement instead of answering the call to become elders. To acknowledge that reciprocity is the lore that governs the life-death cycle and that when we align ourselves to it, we can make wine and wisdom of the first order. Meanwhile, we're postponing the challenges and opportunities that could be won from accepting life's limits.

The cultural mythology of our age says achieving personal wealth and happiness are signs of a successful, well-lived life. And if anyone doubts our generosity, we can always do a little community service for the underprivileged or donate some dollars to a tax-deductible HIV clinic in Africa.

The oddity is that the esteem awarded to civic-minded actions like 'CEO sleepouts' and other charity stunts barely acknowledge the real elders among us—women working two jobs who do the lion's share of cooking, cleaning and childcare. Volunteers donating their time and knitwear to thrift shops. Older people who visit even older people who've been abandoned in aged-care facilities. The couples who make room in their hearts and homes to foster unloved children while raising their own.

If we dare to bring ourselves into serving our children and the world, we can become the heroes we're waiting for—authors of memories and legacies worthy of the great myths of yore.

Private myths, public dreams

> *The universe is the unity of all things. If one recognizes his identity with this unity, then the parts of his body mean no more to him than so much dirt, and death and life, end and beginning, disturb his tranquillity no more than the succession of day and night.*
>
> Chuang Tzu

Back in the day, people didn't count on the world being self-sustaining or autonomous. They held a mythologically informed view that the world and its creatures relied on *them* for their continuance, and that all relationships were harmonised when they were reciprocal and mutually beneficial.

They saw themselves as custodians, not owners, in a world that was vibrantly alive, not merely a storehouse of inert and untapped resources waiting to be exploited.

An example: modern astronomy says the daily 'rise' and 'fall' of the sun happens because the sun-orbiting Earth spins on its axis every 24 hours.

But the sunrise ceremonies of earlier peoples said the rise of the sun wasn't mere physics but the result of human prayers and ceremonies rooted in gratitude, respect and thanks. If humans didn't do their part, the sun wouldn't rise in the morning.

The same understanding of reciprocity and relationship is a hallmark of the rituals and myths of early human culture and some of today's surviving indigenous cultures.

These rituals and prayers often accompanied plant harvesting and the culling of animals for their meat and fur. These were signs that people were conscious of and grateful to living creatures for their sacrifice—or what some called their 'giveaway'.[93]

But there are no such rituals today in the factory farms, slaughterhouses and hydroponic farms that turn animals and plants into the products that fill our supermarket trolleys.

And few in the globalised food system—be they farmers or meat packers or chefs at Michelin-starred restaurants—show any sign of being in a respectful relationship to the creatures they commodify for our appetites.[94] The same could be said of us—the consumers who live in ignorance of what's done to the land, rivers, oceans and creatures we feed on.

A modern person might deride the myths of earlier times as the quaint or ill-informed fantasies of a pre-scientific age. Perhaps the bigger truth is that modern science and information technologies have made us more certain of what we know, but somehow diminished our imaginations and enfeebled our capacity for wonder. Again, Stephen Jenkinson offers this:

'Wonder is the sum of life's way of being itself, washing up on the shore of what you have known until now, leaving handfuls of treasure scattered among the small boulders of what you were sure of. You gather some of that treasure for no reason you can figure without telling anyone and stash it under the pillow of your dreams for a time not quite upon you. Wonder is a willingness, decked out as a skill, to be on the receiving end of how vast the world always is, and how unlike your ideas of how it should be, it often is.'[95]

Old myths taught people respect and reverence for life and the natural world. Like poetry and parables, these old myths weren't concerned with objective truth so much as being pointers to a deeper wisdom about the nature of life, love, death and the unique privileges and burdens of being human.

The myths grew from our longing and wonder. In time they became elaborately sophisticated, distilling wisdom passed down over generations from our ancestors. When these forerunners gazed into the night sky, they confected stories of hunting and love, tragedy and conquest, and the deeds of heroes, villains and gods—all guided by a belief in a pervading moral order.

These people were conscious of their mortality and they made counter narratives to infuse death with hopeful meanings. The Neanderthals, for example, buried their human and animal companions with great care, often bestowing them with elaborate 'grave gear' such as weapons and food and trinkets for their long journey after death.

Likewise, the Dreaming or Dreamtime of Australia's Indigenous people is a grand narrative about life and death and the gods, and their intuition about a hidden world lying behind the physical one.

In this respect, myth-making was our attempt to peer into the unknown—into the great heart of silence—to create meaning from mystery. The perennial myth that came from wondering into the void was the story of a divine realm more powerful and perfect and whole than our own.

But mythology isn't theology. The ancients didn't see their gods or the divine as separate or metaphysical. They felt that gods, humans, animals and nature were inseparable, and that we were all participating in the same drama. According to Karen Armstrong, the main function of these gods was to lift humans briefly onto a more exalted plane of existence so that they could see the world with new eyes.[96]

Enacting these myths through rituals gave people opportunities to experience themselves in ways that reminded them of their divinity. Choreographed dancing, chanting, sacrifices and pilgrimages were ways for people to recall and re-embrace their divinity—and to help them cope with the human condition.

But we're no longer a myth-making people. Why this is so is hard to say, but in a post-religious, scientific age, one result is that we have no stories to bind or carry us on our journey to the grave and beyond.

If Eden's story is a tale of how our unique capacity for thought separated us from nature—when Adam and Eve ate from the tree of knowledge—then our forgotten capacity for myth-making compounds our estrangement.

We've become strangers in a strange land—lonely, thinking animals, living *in* the world but no longer fully *of* the world. Our separation has rendered us homeless, which makes living and dying a hard and sorry business.[97]

Homeless

> *We are here to awaken from the illusion of our separateness.*
>
> Thich Nhat Hanh

One of the unique and troubling challenges of being human is our separation from nature. We harbour this separation in our heads, hearts and souls, a quandary that has rendered us homeless in a most profound way.

Many of us have been physically separated too. For millennia, we've fled our families and homelands due to war, slavery, persecution, migration, disasters and the search for a better life. These experiences are rooted somewhere in our collective memory, and recorded examples go back as far as the Old Testament of the Bible.[98]

By contrast, people with a long intergenerational history of living securely with the land feel deeply at home.[99] Crucially, these people know where the bones of their ancestors lie, and they have a profound sense of belonging to their forebears, to the plants and animals, and to the land, skies and waterways.[100]

Before their culture was disrupted 250 years ago, scholars say Indigenous Australians lived this way for as long as 60,000 years. Their Dreaming mythology infused everything with sacred meaning.

When life is lived mythologically, there's no separation between what we might see as *mundane*—chores, study, work, commuting, food preparation—and what we call *sacred*—prayer, sacrifice and worship.

For many indigenous people, mythology mirrors their deep feeling of belonging to nature: *everything* is sacred, especially hunting, gathering, storytelling, celebration and the initiations that inform their spiritual evolution from birth to death.

Among the many tragedies perpetrated by disruption to indigenous cultures, perhaps the greatest was stealing and removing people from their homelands through the practice of slavery.

Of course, slavery inflicts many more wrongs—it denies people their liberty, their customs, their gods and their language, but its chief injury is to violate people's feeling of belonging by stealing their sense of spiritual and cultural belonging.[101]

Similar wounding has befallen people who've been forcibly removed from their land or who have fled in fear of persecution and death. Some immigrants and their descendants feel a similar deprivation even though they and their forebears weren't stolen or fleeing from calamity.

In the United States, the southern and westward expansions of the frontier that began with the British colonial settlements of the early 17th century created opportunities for immigrants and pioneering settlers to stake their claim for a new home and a better life.

But going west didn't mean they had any idea of how to be at home in their new environment. With their ancestors behind them in Europe or back in the newer colonial settlements to the east, these pioneering immigrants quickly became cultural orphans. They had no lineage, no elders and no mythology to ground them in this new land.

What's more, their loss was bought at the expense of indigenous people. Encouraged by a belief in 'manifest destiny' and the passing of laws such as the *Indian Removal Act* of 1830 and the *Indian Appropriations Act* of 1851, the US Congress extinguished native title to land that enabled the forcible removal of Native Americans from their ancestral homelands to accommodate the European-American expansion west of the Mississippi River.

Indigenous people who agreed to assimilate into the new white culture were allowed to stay on their lands rather than being moved to reservations. But assimilation meant abandoning long-held stories and practices that ruptured their cultural identity.

Anthropologists who study the impacts of human dislocation and ethnic cleansing say it takes just two generations to break the bonds that bind people to their ancestry and their sense of being at home.

'The grandchildren, with no lived or recounted memory of any ancestral home, know nothing of Home—nor do they know that about themselves,' writes Stephen Jenkinson. 'They don't know what the elders are talking about, if they are still talking about what was left behind, and they don't often know much of the language the elders are speaking when they do. What the grandchildren know is flight.'[102]

But those of us with the good fortune to have a house, a passport and citizenship of a nation-state are still cultural orphans with nothing and nobody to fill our longing for a spiritual home.

But home isn't a place or psychologised state of being, even though the real estate and home decorating industries have convinced many that feeling homely signals the bliss of a spiritual home.

Nomadic people have no settled location. They move from place to place as a way of obtaining food, finding pasture for livestock and making a living. Their shelters are temporary, and their movement is guided by the seasons and the availability of plants, game and water. Today, some 30 to 40 million people are classed as nomads, drawing on traditions dating back as far as 8,500 BC.

With no fixed address, nomadic people bear their children and bury their dead by the trail. No headstones or cemeteries mark the whereabouts of their fallen ancestors.

But how is it possible to be at home with no fixed address? One clue lies in the relationship that nomads and some surviving indigenous peoples share with their ancestors. In these cultures, the dead feed the living. When grandpa dies, the tribe honours the old man with days of grieving and stories and songs and feasting.

The old man is present at his wake, propped in a makeshift chair or throne to hear the stories of his life—his achievements and failures. Everyone feasts on the marrow of his life and when the ceremonies are done, they put him in the ground and move on.

But he's not gone or forsaken. Soon after he's in the ground, the old man's body starts to rot through the action of microbes in his body and the bacteria, fungi and worms in the soil. Within three years, his remains have put large quantities of carbon and nutrients into the soil, resulting in lush plant growth.[103][104]

Meanwhile, the old man's tribe continues its journey, always following the herd from pasture to pasture until they stop to settle on the best-eating grasslands, nourished by their fallen elders. All are fed by ancestry and all are nourished by the countless accretions of the dead: the soil, the pasture, the livestock and the tribe.

The wisdom here is that death doesn't rupture relations between the living and the dead but, rather, affirms its necessity for life's continuance and sustenance.[105]

The dead aren't gone, they're present to the living through stories and customs and, most emphatically, as nourishment if we can appreciate and embrace the cycle of life and death. For those fortunate enough to know and hold their ancestors closely, the dead are never lost—they are destiny—and the living are always at home.

But for most of us there's no balm for our loss and no liniment for our fear of dying and death. Without a spiritual home or a cultural context, we seem to be tearing at the world in a frenzied pursuit of what we've forgotten. And all the while we are turning the Earth into a smoking ruin—a stark reminder of our inner landscape.

We belong nowhere. We have no tribe, no elders and no ancestral story to bring us home. No wonder the news of our death has become an existential horror to us. But it wasn't always so, and in some parts of the world it's never been so.

The road from Damascus

Abdullah Kurdi was displaced for a decade before he became the lightning rod for a story of our times.

Originally from Kobanê in northern Syria, he moved to Damascus a decade ago with his brother and father, where he settled in the mostly Kurdish neighbourhood of Rukn al-Din, on the slopes of Mount Qasioun.

Before he moved to Damascus, Abdullah was among the thousands of Syrian Kurds who had sought work in provincial towns and cities across the nation because of the poor job prospects in the country's Kurdish regions.

But when the Syrian civil war began after the Arab Spring of 2011 his life in Damascus became perilous. Struggling to make a living amid the instability brought by the violent protests between the opposition and the Syrian government, he returned to Kobanê in 2012.[106]

There he married his cousin, Rehenna, and opened a barber shop, but struggled to earn a stable income due to the civil war's draining effect on the economy. His income shrank to a fraction of what he made in Damascus, a challenge compounded by the birth of the couple's first son, Ghalib.[107] Unable to pay the rent, Abdullah was forced to close the shop only four months after its opening.

To make ends meet, he left his wife and baby son to take a job in a cement factory in Tal Abyad, a border town 70 km east of Kobanê. When government forces retreated from Raqqa at the end of 2012, the Islamist groups Ahrar al-Sham and al-Nusra Front took control of the strategic border town.

Abdullah was forced to flee again when al-Nusra thugs began persecuting Kurds in the town and its surrounding villages. Returning to Kobanê briefly, he then crossed the border alone into Turkey in search of work and safety from persecution.

He moved into a share-house in Istanbul and worked in a factory 25 km away but struggled to survive because of high commuting costs. He stayed for 18 months and returned to Kobanê every few months to see his family and pass over his tiny savings. During this time, the couple conceived their second son, Alan, who was born in August 2013.

In September of 2014, the situation in Kobanê worsened after the Islamic State militant group launched a major offensive on the city. Much of Kobanê was quickly overrun and Rehenna and her sons joined the hundreds of thousands of refugees that were forced to flee.

While most Kobanês fled to refugee camps in Suruc, close to Kobanê, Rehenna and her sons escaped to Turkey to join Abdullah in the Eyup neighbourhood of Istanbul. There the young family of four scraped by for a year, but their financial situation was precarious with Abdullah doing only odd jobs on building sites.

In good months, he could earn 800 Turkish lira but often much less. To ease their hardship, Abdullah's sister, Tima, who had left Syria for Canada 20 years earlier, wired Abdullah 400 lira a month to pay the family's rent.

With Tima's encouragement, Abdullah and his brother Mohammed made their first effort to enter Europe at the beginning of 2015. Their plan was to make safe passage and then sponsor Rehenna and their children from there.

The brothers tried to cross the sea from Edirne in southwestern

Turkey, but the mission failed when Greek border guards caught them and handed them back to Turkish border police.

After his brother, Muhammad, made a second, successful trip alone into Europe, Abdullah decided to try again. He paid a smuggler $4,000, which his sister had given him, to spirit his young family across the Mediterranean to the Greek island of Kos, and then perhaps to Canada where his sister had applied for their resettlement as refugees.[108]

Like many of the 300,000 refugees who had fled to Europe by water that year, Abdullah and Rehenna knew some of the risks they faced and might have heard of the bodies and debris that were washing up on Turkish and Greek beaches.

But by that stage they felt they had no way to forge a better life than making a ten-minute boat ride across the water.

At 11pm on the evening of 1 September 2015, Abdullah and his family boarded a small, motorised inflatable dinghy on Turkey's Bodrum peninsula. Sixteen people were in the dinghy, which was designed for a maximum of eight. It was one of two boats carrying 23 people that set off that night for Kos.

The water was calm when they set off, but everything changed only five minutes later. The skipper of the little inflatable saw the sea was too rough to make the crossing and tried to turn back.[109]

He panicked when he saw the high waves and jumped into the sea, leaving Abdullah in charge of the steering. Moments later, the dinghy capsized and for the next three hours Abdullah tried to keep his wife and tiny sons afloat in the broiling water.

He thrashed in the darkness, shuttling between little Alan, then to Ghalib, and then to Rehenna. In later news reports, he described lifting his children onto the side of the dinghy and begging them to cling to the deflating vessel, but they slowly slipped from his grasp.[110]

The road from Damascus

Only Abdullah survived. Two-year-old Alan, five-year-old Galip and their mother, Rehenna, were among a dozen people who drowned that night in the black sea. The next morning images of Alan's body, which was found washed ashore, flashed across the world.

Abdullah and his family are part of the biggest refugee crisis the world has seen since World War Two. In 2016, it was reported that 65 million people around the globe were stateless and seeking a new homeland.[111] These individuals were forcibly displaced because of persecution, conflict, violence and human rights violations.

Abdullah fled persecution at home. He sought shelter on an island that didn't want him, and his family died near the shores of a land that perhaps wanted him least of all.

In 2015, worsening conditions for refugees in Syria and the wider region saw a million refugees enter Europe with half this number coming from Syria alone.[112] Nearly all came by sea and that year 3,692 men, women and children perished trying to make the fateful crossing.[113]

By 2019, with Syria's president, Bashar al-Assad, closing in on victory after an eight-year revolt, there were five million Syrian refugees spread across the Middle East and Europe. The regime's use of torture, detainment and industrial-scale death camps means most exiled Syrians are unlikely to return home.[114]

Aid organisations, NGOs and some nations, especially Germany, have opened their hearts and borders to the world's 65 million stateless and homeless people, but too many have turned a blind eye.[115]

Even if all these people find a new home, they will probably never return to the land of their ancestry and their children and grandchildren will lose the stories and language and deep rootedness of home.

*

The atoms that make up our bodies are the same as those that comprise the land, the sea, the air and the cosmos. In the long history of the universe, these atoms have been recycled and reconstituted billions of times and taken form in countless beings and entities.

This means that *we are the world*, but our amnesia and myopia mean few of us realise our intimate connectedness with life and death's eternal truths. The world isn't outside us or separate, it's literally within us. Dissolving the duality that disconnects us from the world and each other is the remedy for rooting out the source of our spiritual homelessness. Dissolving separation and waking up to our true nature reminds us that we are deathless, eternal, whole and always dwelling in our spiritual home.

In reality, we lack nothing and when we wake up to our indivisible nature, we remember that we are the one—*the home we've been longing for*. This awakening ends suffering and fear.[116]

This may sound far removed from the grim fate of Syria's refugees and the millions of people seeking safety and safe passage to a new homeland. And yet finding one's spiritual home is no less difficult, even in the affluent West where most of us are far from persecution and have a roof over our heads.

But increasing numbers of people in the West live in relative isolation, almost never talking to their neighbours or family or friends. Feeling a deep sense of belonging is also a challenge for people living in mega-cities that never sleep.[117] The same goes for billions of people tethered to screens and electronic devices. Too many of us live outside of nature and the rhythms of life that bring grounding, connectedness, wonder and sanity.

If we could only stop distracting ourselves, we might see that our spiritual home is within us and around us, wherever we are.[118]

White Helmets

To save a life is to save all of humanity

Abu Omar

The Syrian civil war is one of 60 major conflicts disrupting the lives of millions of people across the world. Beginning in the Arab Spring of 2011, this multi-sided conflict has spawned a major refugee crisis spreading across the Middle East and into Europe.

So far, an estimated 400,000 people have died in battle and from hundreds of massacres and chemical attacks that have brought untold suffering. The United Nations has launched several peace initiatives to end the conflict, but the fighting continues.

Beginning in 2012, groups of civilians from affected towns and cities started responding to one devastating impact of the carnage—people buried beneath the rubble of buildings destroyed by the bombings and airstrikes.

Officially known as Syria Civil Defence, but better known as The White Helmets, their main activities involve urban search and rescue, medical evacuation, and essential services like reconnecting electricity, giving safety information to children and securing buildings.

They have no connection to political, military or religious groups and their mission is to provide humanitarian aid to anyone in need. Since their humble beginnings, the White Helmets have grown to number more than 3,000 volunteers, including 140 women, operating from 111 local civil defence centres across the country.

Mostly, their efforts involve responding to the aftermath of attacks and bombings. Many White Helmets have put their lives on the line amid sniper fire to rescue the bodies of men, women, children and soldiers so the dead can be given fitting burials. By June 2017, 191 White Helmets had been killed saving the lives of their fellow citizens.

Khalid Farah is a former builder and now a White Helmet living in Aleppo with his wife and two young children. A volunteer for the past three years, he has retrieved countless living and dead people from the rubble in a city that has seen 13,500 people killed and 23,000 injured since the conflict reached the city in July of 2012.

Khalid sees no distinction between his family and his fellow citizens. In an interview in 2013, he said:

'I have a strong belief in my work for the White Helmets. Whenever I'm on a rescue I try as hard as possible to save every person under the rubble, whether they are young or old. I consider them all to be my family.

'I have been with the White Helmets for three years. I have seen many people who have died in bombings. I have also seen many people who were rescued alive. The casualties are rising daily. The bloodbath is not stopping. I'm willing to sacrifice my soul for the sake of my people. This job is sacred.

'A child, even if he is not my son, is like my son. I cannot explain it. As an example, I'll tell you a story that happened to us in Aleppo. Two barrel bombs were dropped in the al-Ansari area.

'The first one left a number of people wounded, but the second barrel bomb killed a lot of people. We went into the area. It was like a small village made of ten houses, and all the buildings had been levelled to the ground. On that day, our work was very hard, and we worked for about 16 hours.'[119]

By this time, everyone was weary, and it seemed impossible that there could further survivors beneath the fractured concrete and rubble. Then Khalid heard a cry. A baby's cry.

'I thought I was being delusional because I was so tired,' he said in a media report. 'I asked my friend, "Will you listen? Put your ear here and try to hear. I think I hear a baby's voice". He said, "Yes, it is!".[120]

'This gave us renewed strength to continue the work. It gave us hope that some people were still alive. After 16 hours under the rubble, a baby less than a month old, still alive, under the dust, under the ceilings that had fallen on him. We called him 'miracle baby'.

'The baby was one week old and at that time my son, Abdul Hameed, was almost two weeks old. I don't know how it came to my mind, but I imagined that this was my son. And I started to cry. I couldn't hold it in, and all my colleagues started to cry.'[121]

Khalid's White Helmet colleague, Abu Omar, was with him when the baby, named Mahmud Ibildi, was rescued. He voiced the same sentiment—that people needing rescue need no qualification.

'Any human being, no matter who they are or which side they are on, if they need our help, it's our duty to save them. Every morning, I wake up and do this because it's my duty, my humanitarian duty. In the White Helmets, we have a motto: *To save a life is to save all of humanity.*'[122]

Consider for a moment—that saving the life of an individual is to save all humanity. In its most profound sense, this means that when I dissolve the boundary of otherness I hold between me and another, I understand that I *am* my brother, my sister and all humanity.

The religious scholar Elisabeth Vasko made the same point with different words when she said, 'to be human is to be a person in relation'. Indeed, it's this social and existential reality that binds us to the lives of everyone, without distinction.

'We are here to awaken from the illusion of our separateness,' said the Buddhist monk, Thich Nhat Hanh. This is the truth that Khalid Farah and Abu Omar know in their bones and which they live each day as a sacred duty.

So, the question is: when I dissolve the boundary that separates me from my neighbour, and come to know that you are my brother, my sister and humanity *itself*, what's my sacred duty?

Initiation

> *Human beings aren't born. Human beings are made. And how do you make humans? Well, you've got to kill off their childhood. Any why? Because the childhood doesn't give way. And then you need a culture that proceeds as if the greatest gift you can give kids at a certain age, is to give them the chance to be human.*
>
> Stephen Jenkinson – *The Making of Humans*[123]

For the most part, we're taught that we're pre-wired to grow from infancy into fully functioning adults. Of course, schools teach us reading, writing and arithmetic to help us on our way, and our parents give us our morals, or try to.

But there are few ceremonies or rituals that properly initiate young people into adulthood. We offer no transformative rites of passage for young people to learn or earn the privileges and responsibilities of becoming a mature human being. Nor do we have ceremonies to teach children about death—theirs or that of their parents and loved ones.

And for the curious few, reading scholarly books on initiatory rites of passage isn't much help. These narratives are often obscure and baffling, perhaps because few anthropologists have experienced these rites. Further, these accounts tend to focus on adolescent rites of passage, but these are merely a prologue to full humanhood, not the whole story.

In fully intact societies, initiations weren't (and aren't) one-off events, but ceremonies that punctuated the lives of humans at pivotal thresholds, including events like menstruation, marriage, conception, childbirth and death. In some Australian Indigenous traditions, women will experience up to seven initiatory rites of passage, and men as many as 13.

Joseph Campbell's writings on initiation are visceral. Writing about male puberty rites that were performed in the Paleolithic caves of southern France and northern Spain around 30,000 BC, he reported this:

'Everything was done, even in the period of the Paleolithic caves, to inspire in the youngsters being symbolically killed, a reactivation of their childhood fear of the dark. The psychological value of such a "shock treatment" for the shattering of a no longer wanted personality structure appears to have been methodically utilized in a time-tested pedagogical crisis of brainwashing ... for the conversion of babes into men.'[124]

These rites were meant to shatter adolescents' immature preoccupations by exposing them to the smell and sound and texture of death. They were exposed to risk and fear to create a vivid belief that they might die during their ordeal in an effort to kickstart a change in awareness they would carry through life.

By doing so, the initiators, who were the elders of the tribe, hoped to make death into something real and knowable instead of something remote and fearful.[125]

These rites of passage were a provocative antidote to the modern-day mantra that says knowing you will die is traumatising, or that end-of-life conversations should be avoided or tiptoed around until 'later', which means never. This belief applies especially to children who, it is argued, should be shielded from knowing and witnessing death, especially their own or that of their parents.

By contrast, the purpose of culturally endorsed puberty rites is to end childhood and start personhood. These rites are meant to forge an ability to prize life and begin a kinship with death that says, 'Your life has limits'.

The French Renaissance writer Michel de Montaigne argued that forging a kinship with death is the path to freedom. He wrote: 'To begin depriving death of its greatest advantage over us, let us adopt a way clean contrary to that common one, let us deprive death of its strangeness; let us frequent it, let us get used to it; let us have nothing more often in mind than death. We do not know where death awaits us so let us wait for it everywhere. To practice death is to practice freedom. A man who has learned how to die has unlearned how to be a slave.'[126]

But today's rites of passage aren't transformational because they don't annihilate the self-absorption of childhood, to say nothing of forging a kinship with mortality.

Our religious and social rites of passage like Jewish bat/bar mitzvahs and Christian confirmation ceremonies are fail-safe rituals.[127] They're relics of old initiatory rites that do nothing to break our attachment to childhood or to set young people on a path to further rites of passage and thresholds of change.

In the West, the mark of personhood is psychological individuation and for the most part we achieve this by defining ourselves *against* our parents and society's cultural norms. This process really hits its stride in adolescence, a phase characterised by rebellion and turning away from parents and all that they represent.

Within limits, this rebellion is accepted as a necessary part of growing up. Bad-tempered, self-absorbed, emotionally petulant teens are tolerated mostly because they're repeating a time-honoured norm that's familiar, even if it's not so welcome.

Some parents probably recognise themselves in their teenager's revolt. Deep down, they might empathise with their kids' cynicism and isolationism because they have started to sniff the world of strife they're going to inherit.

Since 9/11 many of the killings and acts of terror unleashed in Western countries were planned and perpetrated by 'home-grown terrorists'—mostly young men born and raised in the West. More than a few experts have diagnosed the 'radicalisation' of young men as being the root of this phenomenon.

The logic of their argument goes like this: disenfranchised young men are easy prey to the purveyors of radical Islam because they feel isolated and vilified for a host of complex reasons. As a result, their simmering resentments have become fertile ground for sowing the seeds of hostility, retaliation and violence.

Some proponents of this argument say young men at risk of being radicalised should be brought into the fold so that they feel they belong—to understand that they have value and talents that can be put to good use in their communities. So far, so good.

Who should reach out to these young men to bring them back to the bosom of society? Who's best placed to counter the avalanche of radical propaganda pervading social media and the internet?[128]

Some pundits say the job should be done by their politically and socially moderate peers; responsible young men who've crossed the threshold to maturity. Why? Because their elders and community leaders don't understand them—they're out of touch, and can't be trusted, goes the argument.

During the counterculture movement of the 1960s, the student activist Jack Weinberg said, 'Don't trust anyone over 30'—a line that still has currency among commentators who say young men at risk of being radicalised can only be reached by their peers. The generation gap is as old as time itself, no doubt.

As an example of this thinking, Australian journalist Mike

Seccombe and Dr Joshua Roose, a Muslim and research fellow, have argued that socialising young men into moderate, law-abiding behaviour is too important to be left to the oldies.

In a 2015 article, Seccombe wrote, '"For these at-risk young people, the Grand Mufti is an irrelevance," says Dr Joshua Roose, a Muslim and research fellow at the Institute for Religion, Politics and Society at the Australian Catholic University. "Most wouldn't know his name," said Roose.

'The key', writes Seccombe, 'is finding a way to appeal directly to those who are at risk of radicalisation. Working through intermediaries, be they elderly clerics, police or welfare workers, will not do it. What is needed ... is something, someone, to make confused youth "feel Australian".

'"There are several such people out there," says Roose, "—young, educated, articulate, starting to be heard. They will be the key figures in the fight against radicalisation. Not an elderly, largely irrelevant Egyptian bloke."'[129]

So, elders and community leaders over 30 are an irrelevance, goes the argument. They should leave the field of battle. Instead, the critical task of initiating young people into adulthood, of guiding them towards the community and its moral order, and away from the preoccupations and vanities of self-absorption should be left to young people themselves.

Meanwhile, the dearth of transformative initiation rites could be opening a door to all kinds of problems, not only the possibility of home-grown terrorism.

In our culture, adolescent psychological individuation—which means carving out an identifiable 'me'—is done by separating ourselves from our parents, and by turning inward and away from society.

But how do we learn to turn towards another? How do we

tame narcissism so that we can merge with another in intimacy—with our lover, our spouse, our children and our parents?

And how do we begin to have these important conversations about dying and death—ours, and theirs?

To reiterate, in earlier times puberty and other initiation rites were done by the elders of the community—people versed in the wisdom and practice of their lore; those who were closer to death, and who had earned their position through learning and mastery. Grey-haired men and women who'd achieved mature states of personhood and leadership.

These elders held the stories and myths that taught what it meant to live deeply as a human. These stories and myths were handed down through repeated telling and were intended to feed our capacity for wonder—about love, life, the universe and death.

But today we have 'seniors' instead of elders. Our seniors are people whose only qualification for the title is to have lived long enough to attain it. Truth be known, they were probably raised in a culture that gave them a free pass into adulthood, middle age and seniority. But our seniors may be no wiser in the arts of living soulfully or knowing how to initiate and mentor the next generation than the rest of us.

Alchemy is the transformation of base metal into something of value. But our modern coming-of-age rites require no effort or sacrifice, so they don't achieve the alchemy that's necessary to turn children into fully functioning adults.

History has shown that old initiation rites can change our untutored and childish ideas of ourselves into true personhood, thereby fashioning our tiny idea of ourselves into something grander and more valuable—into something infinite and deathless.

Identity

> *In this high place*
> *it is as simple as this,*
> *leave everything you know behind.*
> *Step toward the cold surface,*
> *say the old prayer of rough love*
> *and open both arms.*
> *Those who come with empty hands*
> *will stare into the lake astonished*
> *there, in the cold light*
> *reflecting pure snow*
> *the true shape of your own face*
>
> David Whyte, *Tilicho Lake*[130]

Our fear of death is based on a fundamental misconception about who dies, and what is deathless.

When Descartes said, 'I think, therefore I am', he was equating thinking with identity. Plato ventured the same idea 2000 years earlier and his influence has permeated philosophical thought and Western conceptions of identity ever since. As a result, most of us have an identity that's synonymous with our idea of ourselves. We have little sense that what we call our 'true self' could be anything but this thought-generated identity.

The human mind is a powerful tool with exceptional capacities and achievements to its credit. It has split atoms, created symphonic masterpieces, and flown us to the moon and back. But identifying with thought—the belief that I am my thoughts and my thoughts are always true—creates a filter or screen of ideas, concepts and judgments that hinder a true, direct relationship with the world.

This mind-made identity separates us from our fellow humans and all phenomena by creating an illusion that there is a so-called 'me' and a totally separate 'you' or 'other'. How could it be otherwise? I am here and you are over there, sealed off in another body. The same goes for the rest of the world: trees, animals, rivers and mountains, all of them outside 'me'.

In 1971, the Apollo 14 astronaut Edgar Mitchell had an epiphany about his identity during his return flight to Earth after walking on the moon. Suddenly, his idea of separation collapsed on itself:

'The biggest joy was on the way home. In my cockpit window every two minutes, the earth, the moon, the sun and the whole 360-degree panorama of the heavens. And that was a powerful, overwhelming experience.

'Suddenly I realized that the molecules of my body, the molecules of the spacecraft, the molecules in the bodies of my partners, were prototyped—manufactured—in some ancient generation of stars. And that was an overwhelming sense of oneness, of connectedness. It wasn't them and us—it's me—it's all one thing. And it was accompanied by an ecstasy—oh my god, yes, an insight, an epiphany.'[131]

Some Eastern philosophies argue that thinking and consciousness aren't the same, viewing thought as merely one aspect or element of consciousness. According to this view, thinking can't exist without consciousness, but consciousness—pure simple awareness—doesn't require cognitive thought.

Identity

But the proposition put by several Eastern philosophies that says, 'I am not my mind', has little to no acceptance in Western philosophy. Whether we know it or not, we're all Cartesians.

But this mind-based identity caper has important consequences. It means we derive our sense of self (I am) solely from thinking, which is the genesis of a mind-based self, or ego.

One effect of identifying with our thought-based identity is that it makes thinking compulsive. Why? Because, without it, our identity, our sense of self dissolves. Ego needs thought to exist and non-existence is intolerable to ego because it means the death of self.

Another effect is that egos have no 'off switch' and therefore many of us live with an incessant internal monologue. This constant mental chatter stops a lot of us from experiencing inner quiet or tranquility. All we have is a stream of thought-based consciousness—like having a radio announcer turned up load, endlessly droning in our ear.

This makes it nearly impossible to connect to our deeper sense of self and the wider world. This, in turn, feeds our sense of disconnection, reinforcing a belief that 'I' truly am a separate self, a lonely atomised fragment in a vast and alien universe.

This mind-based identity finds compelling evidence for its existence in the past and the future. It seeks comfort and solidity in biography and memory and past achievements, as well as in its plans and hopes for the future. But death means annihilation for a mind-based, ego-self. If I am my thoughts, and dying terminates body and mind, then death is truly the end of me, right?

The myth scholar Joseph Campbell put it like this:

'The universal self becomes divided immediately after conceiving and uttering the pronoun "I". This illustrates the fundamental Indian conviction that a sense of ego is the root of the world of illusion. Ego generates fear and desire, and these are the passions that animate all life and even all being; for it is only after the concept "I" has been established that the fear of one's own destruction can develop, or any desire for personal enjoyment.'[132]

Likewise, Sogyal Rinpoche argues that our false ego-identity is the root of our fear of death:

'Perhaps the deepest reason why we are afraid of death is because we do not know who we are. We believe in a personal, unique and separate identity—but if we dare examine it, we find that this identity depends entirely on an endless collection of things to prop it up: our name, our "biography", our partners, family, home, job, friends, credit cards ... it is on their fragile and transient support that we rely for our security. So, when they are all taken away, will we have any idea of who we are?

'Without familiar props, we are faced with just ourselves, a person we do not know, an unnerving stranger with whom we have been living all the time, but we never really wanted to meet. Isn't that why we have tried to fill every moment of time with noise and activity, however boring or trivial, to ensure that we are never left in silence with this stranger on our own?'[133]

*

Sometimes we experience moments of silence when the mind stops its internal monologue. This can happen when we're awed by the beauty of nature, absorbed by art, or perhaps if we practice meditation.

When we experience this 'mind gap', we are in pure awareness, unsullied by thoughts, judgments or attitudes. In these moments, we experience another ever-present dimension of ourselves that shines through when thinking subsides.

Identity

Being present without mental labelling can be a deeply satisfying experience. We experience life unfolding, moment by moment, and by so doing we enter the vast, quiet stillness that lies behind mind-generated phenomena.[134] This stillness is available in every moment. Our life is literally happening now, not in the past or the future, so being present lets us catch up with ourselves, and with life.

When we're present to this moment we aren't our ideas or beliefs or mental imaginings. We're not our memories or imagined futures. We're not our opinions of ourselves, or the opinions of others. These are simply thought-based phenomena, not reality, although they often cast a long shadow over our experience of life and our thoughts of death and dying.

The truth is, our mental imaginings have turned death and dying into monsters. Many of us believe these mental phantoms, but their effect is a limitless and unrelenting fear. Imagine your worst idea of your dying and death, and then obsessing over it, forever. That's what many of us have got ourselves into.

And what do we fear?

We fear the pain of dying. We fear writhing in agony. We fear losing control—physically, emotionally, mentally. We fear losing our dignity. We fear being a burden to our families and our loved ones. We fear that we won't be good enough to face dying and death. We fear being annihilated. We fear saying goodbye to everyone and everything that's precious. We fear dying with unfinished business. We fear dying with unresolved arguments.

We fear dying and not being forgiven our wrongdoings, our sins and the pain we've caused so many people. We fear judgment day. We fear hell. We fear dying alone with nobody to hold us or pray for us. We fear dying with an inadequate legacy. We fear being forgotten. We fear dying without tasting the sweetness of life and love we were promised. We fear dying without getting what we came for, what we gave birth for. We fear the unknown. We fear the future.

Life is happening now, and its fullness is available this instant, if we can open to it. Our inexpressible vastness, the true wonder of what we are, is too big for anything we can dream or imagine, and too immense for any thought. But cracking our hearts wide open to life, to this eternal moment, to the power of now, might be our way through.

When dying and death arrive, they'll happen in the present, not the future. Nobody knows the precise details of what these mysteries will ask, but when they come, we can be sure we'll be called to open ourselves in the same way life calls to us *now* to celebrate and marvel at each and every moment.

Living our deepest truth

Eve Ensler rediscovered her calling 20 years ago when she started talking to women about their vaginas. Since then, she's helped women around the world tell their life stories through the untold stories of their bodies. Her play *The Vagina Monologues* has become a powerful force to end violence against women and girls.[135]

The Vagina Monologues and a host of related artistic works have been staged and performed by women in thousands of communities across the world and become a stimulus for educational and community-based anti-violence programs.

An award-winning writer, performer and activist, Ensler collaborates with the V-Day movement to spearhead One Billion Rising, a global protest campaign to end violence against women. Today, the V-Day movement funds over 13,000 community-based anti-violence programs and safe houses for women around the world.

Ensler woke up to her purpose by remembering what she had longed for since childhood. As a young girl she grew up in an upper-middle class white community with all the outward signs of a safe and happy life. But her life was hell. She lived with an alcoholic father who beat and molested her, with all the fear and trauma this brought with it.

She had a fantasy that somebody would come and rescue her and invented a character named Mr Alligator who she implored to save her when life became unbearable. Sometimes she would even pack a travel bag while she waited, hopefully, for Mr Alligator to come and take her away. Mr Alligator never came, but Ensler has said that the *idea* of Mr Alligator saved her sanity. Her fantasy made it possible for her to keep going because she felt someone was coming to her rescue.[136]

The theologian David Tracy says our deepest longing is the root of our purpose and our happiness.[137] We long for love and a context and a community where we don't feel abandoned, as young Eve Ensler did.

When she looked back at her life from middle age, Ensler realised her purpose wasn't something to be sought or found but something she had to recall, something she'd forgotten about her desire to be rescued.

In 2001, Ensler met Agnes Pareyio, a Kenyan woman who has saved thousands of girls and women from being circumcised against their will, as she had been as a ten-year-old. For eight years, Agnes had walked in the Rift Valley of East Africa teaching girls and boys and parents of the semi-nomadic Maasai tribe. Using an anatomical model of a woman's body, she taught thousands of Maasai what a healthy vagina looks like, and what a mutilated one looks like.

She also co-created an alternative coming-of-age ceremony with the Maasai, so that girls could be initiated into womanhood without being mutilated. In those eight years of wandering and teaching on foot, she saved 1,500 girls from genital mutilation.

After meeting Ensler, Agnes was given a jeep to journey deeper into the 6,000 km-long valley. In her first year of using the jeep, she saved another 4,500 girls from being cut and opened safe houses for girls.

When she was invited to the opening of a safe house in Kenya, Ensler realised that through her writing and activism to educate and empower girls and women, she was closing the loop on her own little girl's longing for rescue.

On arrival, she was greeted by hundreds of girls clothed in red homemade dresses, which is the colour of the Maasai and the colour of V-Day. It was a gorgeous day in the African sun. The dust flew as the girls danced and sang about the end of their suffering. Finally, they brought Ensler to a little house draped with a banner that read, 'The V-Day Safe House for the Girls'.

In that moment Ensler knew Mr Alligator had finally shown up. 'He had shown up,' she said, 'obviously, in a form that it took me a long time to understand, which is that when we give the world what we want the most, we heal the broken part inside each of us.'[138]

*

Remembering the particular work we are born for is a hard business today. It's given little comfort or tuition because our culture seems to have forgotten its deepest stories and lessons.

In Greek mythology, the river Lethe was the spirit of forgetfulness and oblivion. It was one of the five rivers flowing through the Greek underworld of Hades, and any soul who drank from the river lost their memory.

The myth is a message from the dead to the living to remember to be human.[139] That we've forgotten how to be fully human is clear from the mayhem in our lives and the chaos in our headlines.[140][141][142] This mayhem and chaos are mirrors of our inhumanity and what keeps us damned, like the souls of Hades, is forgetting what's sometimes too painful to recall. But the painful truth of living, of recalling our hard times and our inhumanity, is the crucible for our compassion and desire to live deeply by responding to our longing.

Each of us is called to particular work, according to our biography and talents and circumstances. Our calling might be being the best, loving parent we can be. It might be achieving our sales targets to give our family a home and financial security. It might be telling stories about the old days to our grandkids.

Answering that call and making it happen in the world is to lay claim to our deepest truth and our kinship to each other. The path to our deepest satisfaction lies in recalling our true purpose and giving the world what we long for as a path to healing our brokenness. It's also a route to becoming fully human and serving each other—a way to bridge the imaginary chasm of separation between us.

Is there anything more important that living your deepest truth?

Pain and suffering

It's no secret that living and dying can be painful. Living provides endless opportunities for learning how to make life less painful, even blissful, but most of us come to dying as amateurs, often unwilling and unready to be sucked into a death spiral we can't control. Ask anyone about their biggest dying fear and they'll tell you it's to be eviscerated by relentless, agonising pain.

And there are good reasons to be scared. Fewer than 20 per cent of dying people manage to shake their body free without a measure of pain and discomfort. Nearly everyone has a nightmare tale of a friend or loved one whose dying days were filled with agony and suffering. We carry these visions and the fear they engender deep in our guts.

So, despite assurances from doctors and palliative care experts who say they can mitigate the pain of advancing disease and the decline of a failing body, nobody should plan on pain-free living or dying. Even best-laid plans can go awry. Murphy's Law is lore because it's true enough.

Dr Sherwin Nuland knew this from long experience and confessed to medicating some of his dying patients to the threshold of death—and over the brink—when he couldn't give them the easy death he'd promised.

In his book *How We Die*, he said: 'In my medical practice, I have always assured my dying patients that I would do everything possible to give them an easy death, but I have too often seen even that hope dashed in spite of everything I try. At a hospice too, where the only goal is tranquil comfort, there are failures. Like so many of my colleagues, I have more than once broken the law to ease a patient's going, because my promise, spoken or implied, could not be kept unless I did so.'

*

The pain of living and dying may be unavoidable, but it's too often hostage to mental anguish that compounds our physical ailments and life circumstances—an anguish we create in our minds and then experience emotionally. This is a double insult but one we needn't suffer, say writers in the Buddhist tradition.

Buddhism has it that our mental anguish is a result of resisting or clinging to people and situations in our life. Add substances to that list too, be it food, booze or drugs. We suffer because we want something we can't have or because we have something we don't want. We're frustrated because we want the sports car we can't afford and we grumble because we're stuck in traffic that's going nowhere. This is no small thing in human affairs—the Buddhists say that releasing our desires and aversions is the hardest work we'll ever do.

In the Buddhist teaching found in the *Sallatha Sallatha Sutta*, the story goes that we suffer when we experience the 'arrows' of life, like criticism, failure, betrayal, and physical hurts. But if a second arrow strikes in the same place as the first, the pain is more than doubled—it's ten times worse, says the teaching.

But this second arrow is self-inflicted. It's the arrow of our reaction, our 'narrative', and the ensuing drama we create that adds insult to the injury inflicted by the first arrow. Self-criticism ('I'm so stupid'), frustration ('This traffic jam is going to make me late for work and make me look lazy'), and boredom ('Ugh, this is killing me. My mother has told me this story a thousand times') are the storylines that fire a second arrow into the painful wounds of living.

The same goes for our physical hurts. My typical reaction to stubbing my toe might be feeling angry or annoyed as I hop about and curse my pain. But this only magnifies the pain by stabbing a second arrow into my hurt and vulnerability. The medicine needed for the stabbing pain is self-mercy, even though I tend to recoil in anger and self-loathing.

So, pain is really a call to soften my heart, not close my body and mind to the experience. Viewed this way, pain is an experience that calls for presence, not fight or flight. Stephen Levine calls this softening 'merciful awareness' and recommends it as a way to restore our capacity for self-compassion rather than condemning ourselves to more suffering.

Of course, it's only natural that pain evokes fears and sorrow, but bringing mercy to these situations can melt our resistance and grow our readiness to trust our intuition for self-healing. In this sense, the pain of living and dying has a kind of moral intelligence because it calls for a willingness to be awake and aware, even when we've learned to hide, numb, repress or condemn our pain.

Levine says our habit of creating fear in painful situations is like desire, except fear lures us backwards to the last 'safe haven' while desire seduces us forward to our next moment of anticipated pleasure. Both reactions lack presence and keep us trapped in a painful cycle of birth and re-birth, pinned to the wheel of samsara. Furthermore, fear and desire often worsen our circumstances because they tend to personalise our pain—which turns it into *my pain*, not *the pain*. This deepens our distress and feeds the illusion that we are helpless victims of our circumstances.

What to do? If we have the courage and insight to forgo these judging and avoidance behaviours, we might see that pain calls us to drop our guard; to enter it directly and go against the teaching of a fear-drenched culture. This seems counter-intuitive—the last thing we've been taught to trust, even though we've seen time and again that avoidance and emotional drama only amplifies our pain by bringing mental anguish to our experiences.

And here's the surprise: opening to pain in the moment can be a revelation. We start to feel and know its features, its colours, its textures. By refusing to label pain as bad or traumatic or inconvenient, we might begin to see it as an experience that invites us to be more complete, more connected to ourselves, rather than fractured. It might be our way home, and a way to live more deeply.

Life presents daily occasions to be present. Garden-variety experiences like low-grade headaches, bodily pains or being stuck in traffic are opportunities to sit with these experiences without commentary or drama and tap into our capacity for acceptance. In the long run, this kind of mindfulness practice might help to build our awareness and mercy for more painful experiences—even the pain that comes with chronic disease and dying.

Being present to pain might also provide insights into our 'unfinished business'—matters of the heart we've avoided or postponed for another time. Life *is* painful, but it needn't be a feared enemy or hateful executioner. What's more, by crafting a relationship with pain before our final days, we might even dissolve the idea that our life is divided between the 'good' bits and the 'bad' bits, the 'boring' and the 'exciting', the 'desirable' and the 'undesirable'—to come home to Shakespeare's truth in Hamlet when he said: 'for there is nothing either good or bad, but thinking makes it so.'

No mud, no lotus

My doctor, Stephen, said he was concerned about my recent blood test results showing a rise in the biomarker we use to track myeloma. In the previous 18 months, I'd had over 100 doses of a chemo drug called carfilzomib. It's for use in patients with myeloma who've had at least two prior therapies but still have disease progression—that is, the insidious, unrelenting disease we call cancer. The rust that never sleeps.

I felt a jolt of panic as he spoke about the recent spike, not because I was overly worried about the uptick—we'd been down that road many times before—but because of his demeanour. Stephen is a world expert in myeloma, and if I was reading his body language correctly, he was agitated by the recent upward trend in the test results. I focused on my breathing and tried not to catastrophise—advice from a book on mindfulness I was reading called *No Mud, No Lotus* by the Buddhist monk, Thich Nhat Hanh.[143]

Nhat Hanh recommends mindfulness as a remedy for suffering and describes a range of tactics to foster more happiness in daily life. In the book's beginning, he points out that despite all the literature and advice on how to cultivate happiness, humans continue to suffer. As a result, many of us believe we're 'failing at happiness' or 'doing it wrong'.

He says most of us don't understand the true nature of suffering and happiness, and he draws on Buddhism's 'four noble truths' to explain the deeper currents of these life experiences. He argues that a more nuanced understanding of suffering and happiness offers many insights, including that suffering is a kind of 'mud' that's essential for deep happiness—hence, 'no mud, no lotus'.

*

Buddhism's four noble truths distil the essence of the teachings of Siddhattha Gotama—the Buddha—who lived mostly in north-eastern India between the fourth and fifth centuries BCE. Briefly, these truths state the following: there is suffering; there are actions that cause suffering; suffering ceases; and, there are actions that end suffering.[144]

Mental and physical suffering is part of life, but we can be so caught in the busyness and preoccupations of life that sometimes we're barely aware of our suffering. And even if our suffering does emerge in ways we can't ignore, such as major pain or strong feelings of grief, anger and anxiety, we have a million ways to distract or numb ourselves against these feelings, especially with painkillers, social media, food and sex. Take a pill. Grit your teeth. Deal with it later. Besides, navel gazing is self-indulgent, for losers, goes the mantra. But denial and running away won't do as long-term solutions given the human condition and the physical realities of life. They're bound to return, again and again.

Furthermore, avoidance behaviours disconnect our body from our heart and head, which means we're asleep at the wheel of life. This separation can put us in grave danger because we fail to notice or deal with our pain, our addictions, our obesity, our depression—until it's too late.

By contrast, mindfulness means being aware of what's happening in the present. It's a way of coming home to ourselves, which, with practice, deepens our understanding and ends our suffering.

No mud, no lotus

Thich Nhat Hanh likens mindfulness to a mother who recognises her baby's cry and cradles it in her arms with love. Being present to our suffering, without judging it or hushing it, is a tender mercy we can give ourselves any time we need it. It begins by stopping, taking a moment, and simply giving our attention to our in-breath and out-breath.

So that's what I did as my doctor pointed at the cancer numbers on his screen and expressed his concern. I kept listening as he talked, but I tuned-in to the sensation of air filling my lungs and letting it go again. No past, no future, just breathing, just dwelling here and now. Doing this reconnected my body and mind in the moment, and despite my doctor's concerns, I felt calm. I was alive and well. What happened with cancer and chemotherapy was something for another time, not now.

When we acknowledge our fears and physical pains, we build our capacity and intuition to heal our suffering, says Nhat Hanh. Doing this means we can learn the art of suffering well—learning how to make the most of the mud in our lives to grow lotuses. Strengthening this skill for mindful self-compassion also means we can bring this balm to the suffering of others.

*

Nhat Hanh says cultivating mindfulness and the happiness it engenders doesn't mean we'll have no suffering at all. But we will suffer less intensely, and less often. Even so-called enlightened people suffer because it's in the nature of humans to create suffering through our endlessly forming desires and attachments. But mindfulness is an antidote because recognising our physical and emotional pain is the beginning of the end of suffering.

Checking-in and being present on a regular basis is the first step. How? Focus on the breath and nothing else. And then notice any sensations in the body. Do I have tension? Aches? Pain? And what am I feeling right now? This mindful noticing is a way to stop being a mindless, disconnected zombie. Our way back to ourselves. A way into the mud of awareness where can I can grow the lotus of understanding and compassion. No mud, no lotus. Without suffering there is no impetus to learn how to cradle ourselves or others, or to grow in joy and wisdom.

Mindfulness also breaks the myth that happiness is something for later, a dividend that's due *after* we've reached our goals—be it the right job, right partner, right house. Will we slog on, wedded to the idea that being happy will have to wait, even though we know plenty of people with all the badges of success who aren't happy at all?

*

Axis mundi is a multidimensional metaphor for the centre of the world and the core of our being. It's the hub of our 360-degree life experience, grounding us symbolically to Earth below and sky above. Like the lotus, we are rooted in mystery and mud but always rising, seeking release, chasing insight and divinity in the heavens, beyond the ground of being. The axis is like the eye of a storm, the point of truth, the quiet place at our centre that if we wander too far can see us sucked into chaos and distraction at the margins.

Myths and religions throughout time have recognised axis mundi in geological features, art, sacred shrines and even in human form. As examples, Japan's Mount Fuji, the Mount of Olives and Calvary near Jerusalem, Mount Sinai in Egypt, and Mecca in Saudi Arabia have come to represent landmarks representing sacred sites or places that hold the powers of nature and the universe. Temples, churches, pagodas and totem poles also suggest a union of above and below, resolving the opposites and contradictions we imagine between male and female, light and dark, heaven and hell, life and death.

Plant symbols are also fertile metaphors for the axis mundi and the resolution of dualities, especially in enlightenment stories featuring the lotus, the Bodhi Tree and the Tree of Life. The cross of Christ's crucifixion is also an axis-tree symbol representing suffering, death and ascension. In a similar way, our bodies have been described as axis or column symbols in disciplines such as yoga, tai chi and meditation. Shamanic myths have also used hollow bones and sacred pipes as axis-symbols—portals that allow communion between the physical and spiritual worlds.

So it's probably safe to say that axis mundi serves many of our hopes and dreams, especially our notions of freedom, resolution, and our experience of the sacred. In this sense, it's how and where we hold our longing and desire for union on the journey home.

End-of-life conversations

End-of-life conversations offer a host of benefits to people facing death, and to their families and friends. They provide opportunities to explore and define the kind of care we want as we approach our last days and moments. These conversations mean confronting the limits of medical and palliative care and the reality that life is finite—facts that trigger mental and emotional alarm for some.[145]

So, it's no surprise that many doctors and patients are cautious when it comes to discussing death, or that many people avoid or delay these conversations till the last minute, or until it's too late.

In a large, often-cited study named *Coping with Cancer*, nearly two-thirds of terminally ill patients said they'd never had a conversation with their doctors about their end-of-life care, despite having just four months to live.[146]

The study also found that the one in three patients who did have end-of-life conversations with doctors were more likely to accept that their illness was terminal. These patients also voiced a preference for treatments that focused on relieving their pain and discomfort in preference to choosing life-extending therapies.

There were other benefits, too. Patients who had end-of-life conversations with doctors were less likely to be resuscitated, had less depression and worry, and were less likely to end up in an intensive care unit or to have aggressive medical interventions near death, such as intubation and mechanical ventilation.

Also, six months after these patients died, their families were less likely to be depressed and felt more prepared for their loved one's death than families of patients who didn't have end-of-life conversations and who endured aggressive medical interventions near death.

Said another way, people who have practical conversations with doctors about their preferences for their end-of-life care seem more likely to die a 'good death' while sparing their families a lot of heartache and distress.

While these findings mightn't be surprising, they're not well known or discussed either in healthcare circles or the wider community. Even if they were, it's still likely that they'd be unwelcome. Our compulsion for finding a fix for death means we're ignorant and afraid to talk about what we might want until it's too late.

Beyond specialties like palliative care, there's almost no discussion about end-of-life conversations. But the costs are heartbreaking. If you have any doubts, watch *Extremis*—a documentary that shows the devastation experienced by three dying patients and their families because they didn't speak up sooner about their life and death choices.

The question is, when your days are numbered, do you want to have serious medical interventions that you didn't choose yourself?

Do you want your kids and loved ones forced to make life and death choices for you, because you didn't speak up sooner?

Do you want them to have to live with the consequences?

Stories about families burdened by making life and death decisions for their loved ones are far too common. So are stories of doctors taking matters into their own hands—sometimes against the wishes of patients and families.

The tragic case of Marlise Munoz, a pregnant 33-year-old

woman, is a case in point. A day after she collapsed at home, Munoz was declared brain dead by doctors. But against her family's wishes, doctors kept her body on ventilators because they said they had a legal duty of care to her unborn 14-week-old baby.

In 2014, teenager Jahi McMath was declared brain dead after complications from what should have been a routine tonsillectomy. Authorities at the Children's Hospital in Oakland wanted to turn off the 13-year old's artificial life support, but her family resisted and transferred her to another facility where her body was maintained by a mechanical respirator.

These examples are just two of many such cases that add to the debate and controversy about defining death, including brain death.[147][148] They also highlight the catastrophic cost of prolonging life beyond its limits despite the high emotional and financial cost to families, health carers and health insurers.

It's estimated that 30 per cent of all healthcare dollars are spent on medical efforts to prolong people's lives—with 80 per cent of that money spent in the final month of life. A lot of this heartbreak and expense happens because most of us haven't made a living will and told someone about it.

Now is your opportunity to speak up about what you want and don't want before it happens. Some people want the full treatment, no expense spared, intervention at all costs. Others want a quiet dignity that spares them from the prolonged pain and trauma that can accompany medical interventions intended to extend people's lives.

The internet makes it easy to create and register a living will (also called an advance care directive) and to appoint a healthcare proxy—someone authorised to make decisions about your medical and end-of-life care if you can't make these decisions yourself.

End-of-life conversations

Advance care directives are meant to advise doctors about what you do and don't want but they are not legally binding in all circumstances or legal jurisdictions.

For example, In the Australian state of New South Wales, the NSW Supreme Court has said that valid advance care directives must be followed. This is because they are a part of a person's right to make decisions about their health.

If an advance care directive is valid, it must be followed. Health professionals and healthcare proxies have no authority to override a valid advance care directive.

In New South Wales, a treating doctor will consider your advance care directive to be valid if three conditions are met: you had mental capacity when you wrote it; it has clear and specific details about treatments that you would accept or refuse; and, it applies to the situation you are in at the time.[149]

Advance Care Planning Australia has a multi-language online resource library containing information, forms, case studies, articles, videos and fact sheets to assist advance care planning.

If we all talked to our family about our choices and completed advance care directives, we could lighten the load for everyone—not least for ourselves, but especially for our loved ones.

Competence

From the cradle to the grave, competence is a highly sought and valued quality in our culture. From toilet training, to first words, to the taking of our first steps, we're applauded for seeking and achieving competent independence. Schooling and education go the same way. The badges of success go to the students and scholars who ace their exams and graduate with honours and prizes.

At work we value the specialists, the experts, the top-flight professionals and artisans who are rewarded with money, titles, status and promotion. For the most part, we live in a meritocracy even though climbing the corporate ladder is easier for white, able-bodied, heterosexual men who went to the right schools and made the right connections.

Our workplaces say they want 'well-rounded individuals', but those that really get ahead are the specialists who keep their heads down and stick to what they know. Work wants experts who are reliable and independent, efficient and effective. Bosses have no time for the amateur or the novice, and any wider learning you do should happen in your own time, on your own coin.

But for most of us who work long hours in one, two or even three jobs to make ends meet, making the time to cultivate our interests and capacities almost never happens. Chores, family, socialising and sleeping gobble up most of our down time.

But our store of knowledge and well-honed work competencies don't serve us so well in human affairs or the messy business of dying. Out intimate relations aren't the same as our workplace and professional dealings. Intimacy wants honesty, openness, trust and vulnerability.

So, when the news comes that you, your partner or a loved one has a life-limiting or terminal disease, professional competencies aren't much needed. What's your job then? What's called for is the raw, unvarnished, unrehearsed version of you.

This is life nudging you towards something you've little to no experience or competence in—inviting you to enter the unvisited and maybe naïve parts of yourself. Engaging in the messiness we feel in the face of uncertainty, and maybe the grief and anger that arrive when people are dying, is a kind of initiation, a descent into the unknown.

But our culture of competence is never far away, tugging at us, ready to take over with its expert opinions and definitive advice. So, when illness and dying come, it's easy to be swept aside by the tide of clinical professionalism that attends the scene in our hospitals and hospices.

For dying people and their families, losing competence is often viewed as a loss of dignity and a diminished quality of life. But losing competence is the inevitable journey of ageing, disease and death. This is the way of it, and it calls for acceptance and compassion, not expertise.

But competence is heady medicine. It says there's no need to suffer, sweat, struggle or die an undignified death. Competence says you can keep your shit together and die without dying.

The mantra of competence feeds the illusion that we were *always* in charge, always driving the bus of life, and that we can do so right up to the end—or until the last possible moment when, maybe, it's finally okay to 'give up' without feeling we've let down the team.

Competence says you should fight terminal illness and dying no matter what. It says being sick or dying too obviously is for schmucks and losers—that sickness and dying are private, even shameful, and come what may, you should keep up appearances for the sake of the kids and the family.

Dying people, says Stephen Jenkinson, are broken-hearted people who don't know how to be heartbroken: 'Their hearts were broken by the news of their disease and by how their citizenship in the Land of the Living slipped a little at a time without them having a vote on whether or how that would happen.

'Their hearts were broken by the treatment options offered to them and by the outcomes of those treatments. They were broken by the confusion, turmoil and quiet distance making that befell their families, and they were broken by their own.

'The answer a death-phobic culture has to the broken-heartedness of dying people is less heart, less broken-heartedness. That is what sedation and antidepressants are designed for, to compromise dying people's capacity to suffer. This compromise is their great victory, to ratchet down suffering by compromising someone's capacity to suffer.'[150]

What's it like to live with a disease that will shorten your life?

How does it feel when your strength and stamina and resolve to show up for duty in the land of the living starts to fade and flag?

What's it like to die?

No healthy living person is really qualified to answer these questions, but the alternative to dying quietly and calmly and unobtrusively—or being a compliant accomplice to competent dying—is a revolutionary idea in a death-phobic culture.

What if dying and death were schools for life?

What if we took a view that knowing and witnessing and

speaking about dying and death were opportunities to learn, well beforehand, what these events require?

Getting good at the changes that come with dying, like pain and losing control over the body, means the surrender of competence and the collapse of hope.

*

Six years ago, I witnessed my mother dying from complications arising from a heart-valve procedure. Her kidneys were failing, and she was suffering immense pain from clots in her legs despite the opioids she was being given every four hours.

She knew she was dying so when she could summon her strength, we shared old stories and talked at length about how she felt about dying and her looming death. I talked about my grief and my fear and my broken-heartedness. Between us, we made a place for suffering and sorrow and a love that could foresee its own end.

The intimacies of her dying will always be with me, but three memories stand out. Each time I was with her she asked me to wash and wipe her face and body, to comb her hair, and to hold her gnarled hand as she rode the pain that bucked and rocked her body.

Asking to be cared for in these intimate and personal ways was the mark of the woman: she'd never been too proud or vain to ask for help when she needed it, and it was a sign of her trust and acceptance of what was unfolding. For me it was a privilege, a treasured gift.

Before dying became a medically shrouded and private affair, it was an occasion for people near and far to pay their respects and to do whatever needed doing. It was a messy, crowded domestic event involving anyone who wanted to lend a hand or witness the dying of a friend or loved one.

It was the antithesis of competent dying because it was a recognition that the community had the dying person in its many and capable hands. There was no need for a dying person to keep up appearances. No need to say, 'I'm fine, I got it'. No need to die without dying.

A lifelong Catholic with an unshakable faith, Mum had no doubts about where she was heading. She'd abandoned all hope of averting her death and she was running headlong towards it.

This was an immense relief for me and eased the sadness we both felt in her final days and hours. The day before she died, she opened her eyes and said, 'I'm turning away from the world now because I'm turning my face to God. I hope you understand because I don't want you to feel upset or afraid.'

I knew then we were no longer on the same path. In fact, she'd probably turned on to her own path much earlier, when she'd said her prayers before going under the knife for the heart procedure.

Sitting by her warm, lifeless body the next day, I howled in grief and gratitude for what she'd endured and shared and taught me about dying with an open heart. She'd spared us both from the curse of competency. And by abandoning hope and candidly inviting me to witness and aid her dying with all its suffering and loss, she'd led me to experience everything I felt without reserve.

Her gift was to feed me a little of my own death, so I'd have something to nourish me when I got there.

I prayed my grief would never leave me. I didn't want to be fixed or mended or healed because I knew the price of getting over my sorrow would be a kind of amnesia about what it meant to be fully human.

So, I vowed to make a home for it, sensing that my broken-heartedness would keep me awake and maybe more useful in the world.

Euthanasia

Euthanasia is the practice of intentionally ending a life to relieve pain and suffering.

Definitions of the term vary and overlap with a host of related practices that include assisted death, physician-assisted death, aid in dying and suicide.

While these terms mean different things *at their margin*, I'm using them here to mean the *same* thing because of what they have in common—actions that hasten death, most often used by individuals with chronic, terminal or insufferable conditions.

The availability of euthanasia varies from place to place, depending on religious, legal and moral factors. It's worth teasing out these factors to examine the thinking of those who would deny or enable others the right to end their own lives. It's also worth going beyond our judgments and critiques to probe deeper. What's true when we put aside our self-appointed right to judge those who want to end their life?

*

Euthanasia is categorised as a voluntary, non-voluntary or involuntary act and further divided into passive or active variants.

Passive euthanasia causes death by withholding a life-saving treatment like chemotherapy or turning off life-support mechanisms such as mechanical ventilators that are necessary for continuing life.

Sometimes known as 'pulling the plug', voluntary euthanasia is legal under certain circumstances in many countries around the world

Passive voluntary euthanasia means that a person has *consented* to life-ending actions, usually as a result of end-of-life discussions with their doctor and/or family.

It can also take effect through an advance care directive, in which an individual has given written consent authorising someone to make end-of-life decisions on their behalf, if they're unable to make the decision themselves.

Non-voluntary euthanasia is done when obtaining a patient's consent isn't possible, usually because they're in a coma or perhaps suffering from an advanced neurological disease, such as one of the dementias.

These decisions are usually made by a patient's family in consultation with a doctor in the absence of an advance care directive. These scenarios are always difficult and often protracted, and usually compound the grief of loved ones.

Involuntary euthanasia occurs when euthanasia is done without informed consent, either on a person who doesn't want to die, or who wasn't asked.

Active euthanasia involves the use of lethal substances that are usually injected to cause death. It is highly controversial and legal in only a handful of countries, such as Belgium, Canada, Switzerland and the Australian state of Victoria.

Active euthanasia is a form of assisted suicide. It means the suicide is done with the aid of another person, usually, but not always involving a doctor—a practice called physician-assisted suicide.

Individuals who want an assisted suicide that's approved by the state need to qualify by satisfying many criteria, such as having a terminal illness, proving they're of sound mind, voluntarily expressing their wish to die, and taking a specified, lethal dose of drugs themselves. A doctor's assistance is usually limited to writing a prescription for lethal drugs.

Exit International is an international organisation advocating the legalisation of voluntary active euthanasia and assisted suicide.

Because active voluntary euthanasia is only legal in a few countries, Exit International supports people who want to kill themselves by providing information about how to procure lethal substances that cause a quick, painless, peaceful death.

The organisation was founded by Dr Philip Nitschke, who was the first doctor in the world to administer a legal, lethal voluntary injection under the short-lived *Rights of the Terminally Ill Act* in Australia's Northern Territory.

*

People living with chronic or terminal conditions have a host of reasons for wanting to die before death claims them.

Their leading motives include loss of autonomy, a dwindling ability to engage in activities that make life enjoyable, loss of dignity, intolerable pain from their disease or medication, loss of sense of self, and a fear of burdening others. Other common reasons include long-standing beliefs in favour of hastened death, a desire for control, and people's fears about their future quality of life and dying.[151][152]

I remember my dying mother many times saying, 'I wish they'd shoot me,' because her pain was being so poorly managed. She was a lifelong Catholic, opposed to euthanasia.

Throughout her life she'd often said she hoped to face the pain of dying with dignity. She wanted to 'offer up' her pain to Jesus because 'he'd suffered so terribly on the cross'. This might be her way, she thought, to honour his sacrifice. Her way to suffer some measure of his suffering.

She got her wish, but not in the way she'd imagined. She endured persistent catastrophic pain for a week or more before a blot clot lodged in her lung and killed her. But her pain and suffering had been entirely avoidable. Or so I was told shortly afterwards by a palliative care specialist at the hospital.

Before she died, Mum was managed by two teams of specialists—a cardiac surgery team and a renal team. While each was focused on her signs and symptoms, nobody was especially interested in her pain. After all, she wouldn't die of pain, would she? From a medical viewpoint, it seemed like pain was just a regrettable and unavoidable part of her condition.

Both teams knew she had irreversible kidney failure and would die from renal failure within a fortnight. Both knew she had an embolism lodged in her femoral artery that might shift and kill her by lodging in her lungs or brain before she died of renal failure.

Yes, she was being given clot-dissolving drugs. Yes, she was getting opioids for the pain. But she was still suffering. The analgesics she got every four hours weren't doing the job—the dose didn't seem high enough or frequent enough to keep her comfortable. Or maybe she wasn't on the right drug.

Despite my pleading and cajoling, the professionals responsible for her care weren't mobilised by her pain, which is often the case.[153]

The palliative care specialist who spoke to me later said Mum's care should have been managed by a palliative care team. They would have 'coordinated' her care in a way that ensured that all her symptoms—and especially her pain—were well managed.

This was cold comfort. She'd suffered excessively and

needlessly. She'd writhed in pain for days on end to the point where she couldn't focus on dying.

She was agitated and distressed to the point where she couldn't engage properly with family and friends who wanted to support and comfort her, and the many people who'd come to say final farewells.

For days and nights on end she thrashed in terminal neglect and despite all the skills and resources available, nobody took point to aid her. Her dying, and what should have been a rare and exquisite anteroom to death, was obliterated by pain.

So, going against her lifelong religious beliefs, and her desire to offer up her suffering to God, she wanted a quick, assisted death. But in the end, she had no way of taking matters into her own hands, or of empowering anyone else to help her die quickly.

*

The main reasons some of us are opposed to voluntary active euthanasia coalesce around issues of vulnerability, access and concerns about eroding the value of human life.

Once we let doctors kill patients, or help patients kill themselves under certain circumstances, some say there will be pressure to extend the range of circumstances where euthanasia is permissible.

This is sometimes called a 'slippery slope argument' because it's argued that it's easier to amend or liberalise existing laws that permit euthanasia than getting it approved in the first place.

Once active euthanasia is legalised, opponents say that frail, chronically ill or terminal people will be vulnerable to an ever-expanding set of circumstances where doctors could kill patients, or where they could help people kill themselves.

Therefore, patients who don't really want to end their lives might feel pressure to end their lives when this isn't what they really want.

Another rationale used by some opposed to euthanasia is that pain isn't a sufficiently good reason for anyone to want to die. Pain is simply part of dying and can be adequately managed, they say.

Another view is that passive euthanasia is a better alternative—such as withholding life-saving treatment like chemotherapy or turning off life-support systems.

Embedded in this argument is a view that the difference between active and passive euthanasia is morally significant. That letting nature takes its course (passive euthanasia) is morally defensible, while taking a life (active euthanasia)—even with patient consent under legally defined circumstances—is not.

Judeo-Christian religions oppose euthanasia and assisted suicide on moral grounds. The Catholic Church considers active euthanasia to be a 'crime against life' and a 'crime against God'.[154]

Catholicism says euthanasia is a sin because life is 'holy' and 'sacred', and human actions that cause death, or that intend to, are effectively 'playing God'.

Implicit in this view is the idea that God created life and that human actions to end it go against God's dominion and what Catholics regard as the inviolability or 'sanctity of life'. The Jewish, Islamic and Hindu faiths also look gravely on active euthanasia.

*

Euthanasia is divisive. And like other issues that divide us, like immigration policy or same-sex marriage, I'm guessing that people with little to no experience of euthanasia have more strident and negative views than those with personal and professional experience of it.[155]

I say this because there's good evidence, for example, that

people with racially and ethnically diverse social networks are *less* likely to support racist views than people with monocultural networks. Turns out that education and life experience breed tolerance and compassion.

Tolerance says, *I am willing to accept difference. I still have my opinions but as a mark of respect, I am willing to say live and let live. Each to her own. I can agree to disagree and leave it at that.*

Compassion goes deeper than tolerance because it walks in the shoes of another without judgment or opinion. Compassion is a matter of heart, not head, and bridges the divide between us. Compassion says, *I feel what you feel. And even if I thought you were making a 'mistake' by choosing to die as a way to end your fear and suffering, who am I to judge?*

We all face death. Can we be so certain, so righteous in our views that we feel ordained to tell others how to face theirs? What gives any of us the right to tell another that they don't have the right to die?

If we lay aside our arguments and religions and moral precepts, maybe we can let others face these end-of-life choices in their own way.

Orphan wisdom

'Just a sharp scratch,' says Kate, my nurse, as she lines up the vein on the back of my hand and pushes in the needle. A tell-tale spurt of blood shoots into the cannula, signalling that she's hit the mark.

She slides the needle further in and tapes it down. Methodical and efficient as always, she releases the tourniquet, connects the IV line and sets the roller clamp to control the flow of chemo into my body.

Kate has been doing jewellery making of late and we pick up the conversation from last week.

'How's your jewellery-making coming along?' I ask. She tells me about her latest designs and as she does so, she turns her head and tucks her hair behind her ears, revealing her latest pair: navy and sky blue studs encircled in silver.

'I love them,' I say. 'You're a talent, aren't you?'

Smiling, she brushes off the compliment as another nurse joins us to double-check the drug and dosage.

'Name and date of birth, please Daniel,' says Kate. 'Any allergies?'

After five years of this routine, it's easy to lose sight of the fact that the humdrum of this twice-a-week procedure is keeping me alive.

*

The Chris O'Brien Lifehouse in Sydney is a specialist cancer hospital. Opened five years ago, it provides surgery, radiotherapy and chemotherapy for every cancer known to medicine.

Orphan wisdom

The chemotherapy wing sees a hundred patients a day, sometimes more. We sit in the day-therapy waiting room furnished with modern décor chairs and couches lined in rows. They face a wall-mounted screen that mutely shows a news channel depicting the latest tragedy, the newest outrage. Tornadoes in America's Midwest. Riots in Caracas. Presidential hush money to silence a porn star. Clear felling in the Amazon.

A few people hover at the jigsaw table, murmuring over puzzle pieces. Others knit or read or flick at their phone screens. Some people are visibly dying, their bodies ravaged by unrelenting malignancy as their eyes mirror their astonishment at their devastation, their ruin. We all see—imagining, projecting ourselves into their shrunken frames—their withering claim on life. Of course, we can't really know their atrophy but our prayers and hearts reach out.

Others bear the implosive signs of chemotherapy and countless other incursions made to slow or kill cancer. To put off a future nobody wants. Pain and discomfort are writ on bodies and faces. Brightly coloured bandanas are common among the women who've lost their hair, though a few display their baldness with naked pride.

Some of the newly diagnosed patients weep openly as they're comforted by supporting friends and family members. Like the trees and cars and houses on the TV screen, sucked into the vortex of a Midwestern twister, they're in the maelstrom, somewhere between disbelief and terror. There's a grim determination here, tempered by an awareness that our fates are in the balance. Some of us won't make it to Christmas, despite the legions of drugs and prayers and 'stay-positive' attitudes many put their faith in to boost their odds.

The atmosphere is familial in the day-therapy suites where

we get our chemo. There's a cabal of good-natured Irish and Canadian nurses here. They greet each of us by first name and bring humour and humanity to the suffering around them. There are 44 suites, side by side, all of them occupied throughout the day. Clinical conversations bounce along the corridors, each of us hearing our neighbour's story as the nurses deliver our drip-fed remedies.

Once in a while we hear a clanging bell accompanied by cheers and laughter—a ritual to mark a patient's last dose of chemo because they've grasped the holy grail: remission. Cancer free, for now. It's a reminder of why we're here—of what we think we want in a world where 10 million die each year from cancer.

*

What do you when you're not dying, not cured, not in remission? How do you proceed, knowing you'll likely die one day of cancer, but don't know when?

Keep working to pay off the house? Work part-time? Stop work altogether and live off your meagre savings while you have reasonably good health? What if you don't die on schedule and outlive your savings?

And if you did take early retirement, how would you fill your days when most of what you've done for the past 40 years is work and save and raise a family?

What's your purpose if you're not content with gardening and golfing and book club? More to the point, *how could you be content* with these occupations when there's a crying need for elders, people not just seasoned by life experience but individuals stirred by an awareness that they're the beneficiaries of life.

These were questions I faced after five years of chemotherapy. Not sick, not in remission, definitely not dying. But exhausted. Five

Orphan wisdom

years of chemo and continuing full-time work were grinding me down. By the end of the working week I had no energy and I was spending my evenings and weekends simply recovering and sleeping to steel myself for the week ahead.

If I stopped full-time work, I had enough savings to pay the mortgage and maybe last me four or five years—time and space in which I could make myself more useful by dedicating myself to a raft of what I thought of as eldering projects—teaching, community-building and sustainability initiatives that I'd been coaxing along in my spare time.

*

Once upon a time we had elders, people whose words and deeds revealed the wisdom of living and dying in accord with the time-tested truth that life has limits. Elders are antimatter to the financial and economic ideologies of exponential growth and geometric progression. Instead, they're aligned with the everlasting cycles of birth, bloom, maturity, ageing and death.

More than that, they bring us the old story of ancestry, whispering from across the generations, reminding us that we *are* life—and heirs to the generative power of death. These elders are custodians of the past, reminding us of what it means to be human in an age of amnesia—fixated on evermore.

They remind us that our kinship and lineage is grounded in the comings and goings of countless animations reaching back four billion years.[156] They are living testaments of the truth that life will continue even though we won't, and that our lives are nourished and sustained by a non-negotiable covenant of reciprocity.

But our elders are thin on the ground, casualties of a globalising culture hooked on potential and progress, on a credo that says tomorrow has to be bigger and better, no matter the cost. I felt this eldering in my bones and wondered if I had the nerve to sever my own ties to attainment and acquisition.

While I deliberated the question—whether to keep working, to keep slogging away in return for another pay cheque to ensure my financial wherewithal—I succumbed to a seasonal bout of flu. I was never sicker or more moribund. If I needed reminding that I was vulnerable, immunocompromised, living in a body with few natural defences, the flu shook me awake and took me to ground zero.

Lying low for the next few weeks, I came to a resolution. I decided to junk a cargo of long-held attachments. I served notice on my secure, superannuated job. I terminated toxic relationships. I spiked my social media subscriptions. I surrendered a stack of possessions. More than that, I resolved to turn my back on my long-term preoccupation with procuring a confident, cashed-up future, knowing this was an addiction that kept me from my calling, my longing. To step into eldership.

*

In my dreams, Maya, the goddess of illusion, was still cooing. Without me noticing, she'd moved in and cozied up under the doona. She was nestling, like she always did—hot and warm and close.

'You know you need me,' she said, nuzzling my neck, nipping my ear.

Maya was a long-time love. We'd tossed and tangled for as long as I could remember—textbook co-dependents with illustrations.

'Maya,' I said with my most earnest face, 'it's over.'

But she was grinding me. Coming in hot.

'Maya, we have to end this,' I begged, convincing neither of us. We were in a taxi, lit by neon, heading downtown. I caught the taxi driver's glance in the rear-view.

'Brother, you are screwed,' he said with his eyes. 'From here to eternity.'

The air was chilly as we left the cab and I felt sobered as we walked the sidewalks of the city, heading to a dissident dance club Maya had in mind. At that hour, King Cross was beyond description. Junkies, dealers, pimps and prostitutes, plying their trades on Darlinghurst Road and everywhere adjacent.

Maya hugged me close, her foxy fur feathering the night light. Bellhops and bouncers smiled and nodded as we passed. At her, not me. Soon enough, we came to an anti-establishment on Macleay Street. A hulking doorman demanded our credentials, proof of our *bona fides*. Maya shot him a look and we were in, admitted to a denizen where I had no cred, no qualification. The generation gap is real.

'Tonight's the night,' she said without a trace of Rod Stewart irony.

'Hell's bells', I thought, 'I'm in deep. It's midnight and I'm stranded in The Cross, somewhere between the devil and the deep blue sea. And Maya isn't taking no for an answer.'

Truth be known, Maya is a disco queen. She's funk. She's trance. She's dub and she's ghetto, and she danced with a reckless abandon that drew everybody to her like a magnet. I slipped away to the bar to consider my options. Three seconds later, I was out the door, fleeing main street, heading for the hills, somewhere Maya had no purchase on me.

*

Six months after I'd broken up with Maya and stopped working, I had joined the local ranks of retired folks, most of them 'baby boomers' in the over-55s club. Expecting them to be cheerful and grateful at their good fortune, I was astonished at the resentments they harbour. This is the generation that never went to war, and thanks to the counterculture of the '60s and '70s and the reforms of the Whitlam government of the era, it was the first cohort in Australia to get free love (the pill), free tertiary education and free healthcare.

Twenty years later, just as they were taking the reins of power and privilege, the socially and economically progressive Hawke-Keating government introduced industrial and financial reforms that have profited the nation ever since. Australia, the lucky country, has seen 26 years of unbroken economic growth since that time.

A land blessed by peace, prosperity and mineral wealth, it is a social and economic miracle with a robust democracy, a healthy fourth estate, and ever-rising property prices. In the decade since the global financial crisis, one that coincided with the boomers' peak earning capacity before retirement, the stock market, where most of their superannuation is invested, has risen 94 per cent.[157] In other words, the boomers have done well.

So, I was unprepared for their litany of grievances, especially concerning their wealth but also, more predictably, their complaints about the decline in morals and law and order. Their complaints are heard in coffee shops and golf clubs and on talkback radio around the country.

Some context. Current historically low interest rates mean boomers' nest eggs aren't growing as promised. The magic of compounding interest isn't so magical when central banks have set cash rates at somewhere between zero and one per cent. Also, a flattening property market means their million-dollar homes—tax free when they sell—and their tax-friendly negatively geared investment properties aren't skyrocketing in value, as they have for the past 30 years. But it's not all bad news: Australia's dividend imputation laws mean the cheques from share portfolios come tax free.

In Australia's general election of 2019 the progressive Labor Party promised to reform dividend imputation and negative gearing rules that would have removed the tax advantages conferred on people with shares and investment properties. Labor's plan was to redirect the extra tax income to fund more schools and hospitals for the greater benefit of all. The plan would effectively transfer billions of dollars from a smaller wealthy cohort, largely conservative voters, to a larger less wealthy group of people, largely progressive voters. The proposal seemed like smart politics and an opportunity to assist younger, less wealthy people.

The conservative incumbent Liberal-National coalition government promised to leave the tax rules in place and ran an effective scare campaign against Labor's plan that saw the conservatives returned to government for another term. They won government thanks to the ageing, retiring boomer generation who voted for their own continuing financial self-interest. On the first day of trading after the election, the Australian Stock Exchange saw its biggest rise in 11 years, adding $33 billion to its market capitalisation. Banks, mining and property companies, where the boomers are invested, were among the biggest winners.

Most of all, retiring boomers resent ageing and the physical encroachments of growing old.[158] In my neighbourhood, pelotons of middle-aged and older men wearing Lycra rise early to cycle hundreds of kilometres each week. The 24-hour gymnasiums and yoga studios and bushwalking clubs are replete with grey-haired people pushing away their evanescence. Of course, all this activity is admirable and even desirable in the interests of public health in an age of ballooning obesity and heart disease, but it feels more like muscular denial. Sequestered in well-healed suburbs, cloistered in their holiday houses by the coast, cosseted together on their over-55 travel tours, they've all but shrugged off any sense of duty to the younger generations behind them.

They will not give up or give way or give over to those who need them most. Sure, they might be helping out the kids and grandkids with financial leg-ups into property and doing a day or two of babysitting, but for the most part, they are *in absentia*, unavailable to legions of young people seeking support and sustenance from a generation that has long been on the take—on the receiving end of their dumb good luck—who should by rights have learned the rites and rituals of elderhood.

This sounds like censure but it's not meant to. Most boomers, and the remnants of the preceding pre-World War II generation, are uninitiated individuals with no cognisance of the old story that they are heirs to the death-begetting-life-begetting life cycle, or the lore of limits—the covenant of reciprocity that requires giving away all we've been given, including, especially, any wisdom we might have acquired along the way.

Some older people are waking up to their elderhood, but if the vanishing of elders is any measure, it's a rare epiphany. For those who can hear young people's longing for wisdom, they recognise it as a petition to step away from cosy retreat and into servant leadership. Stephen Jenkinson calls this new awakening among our too few elders 'orphan wisdom'. It's an orphan because it has no lineage, no ancestors.

Unfinished business

Dying doesn't have to mean foreclosure or that our last days are congested by regrets, or unspoken words and unrequited feelings.

But in a death-phobic culture many of us live and die with great stores of unfinished business. The result is too many of us feel incomplete when there's so much more to be said and done. This matters because when our love and anguish and gratitude die unborn, we fail to become who we truly are.

We live life seeking connection, understanding, fulfilment, joy and love, and we measure the quality of our days by them. But if our life is ruled by what's in our heads, which serve us so well in our worldly endeavours, we run the risk of dishonouring our hearts.

Stephen Levine has said that embarking on what he calls a 'life review' can be a spur to our awakening and healing.

A life review isn't so much an appraisal of past events so much as a stocktake of our lingering feelings—an acknowledgment of our good works and the healing that could be ours if we were more courageous, more heartful—an opportunity to claim our birthright by bowing to the truth that there's no one more deserving of our love and mercy than ourselves.

'Let us not wait to review our lives on our deathbed,' says Levine.

'Consider the possibility of finishing your business before your lease is up. Don't allow the mind that is so scared of death—of life—even of its own shadow, to make the decision about clearing the future by cleaning up the past.

'Offer that decision to your heart. The heart that has so often been obscured by unfinished business. Offer it the option of finishing farewells, honouring friends and teachers, directing forgiveness to some, and asking for it from others.'[159]

Levine offers specific guidance on how to acknowledge these lingering feelings:

'Sit quietly for a while and bring to mind someone from your past whose kindness touched your heart. Envision yourself speaking to that person. Tell them what they have meant to you. Send your gratitude to them as though your hearts were connected. Thank them, and, when the conversation ends, bid them farewell. Say goodbye to them as if you might never see them again, even in memory.

'Bring to mind, one by one, and without haste, the friends, teachers, parents, ancestors, comrades, lovers and even pets with whom you feel a kinship, those who have supported the growth of your heart. Tell them how much you appreciate their care and kindness. Send gratitude into their image.'[160]

Expressing gratitude for the gifts bestowed by parents, friends, teachers and loved ones can be a beautiful way to acknowledge our abundance and to honour our indebtedness.

Another is to seek the healing that comes from forgiving ourselves and others for the pain we've caused through our unconsciousness—and to clear the debris that still blocks our heart from opening fully.

Levine has offered the following meditation on forgiveness as one way to finish our unfinished business:

'Bring to mind someone who has caused you pain. Not the worst offender, but someone for whom you feel more a sense of resentment than hatred or rage. Someone whose memory is unpleasant but not so anger-inducing that you cannot soften your belly to their recalled presence.

'See how far away from their heart that person must have been to treat you that way, how numb and frightened.

'Just for this moment, as an experiment in healing, touch them with the possibility, no matter how slight, of forgiveness. See how that feels. Notice how the heart longs to be free of its grief. Let it go. Open the fist in which this memory is grasped. Let it float a little freer in the possibility of forgiveness.

'There is a humility to forgiveness that serves well the forgiven as well as the forgiver. A crucial step in self-forgiveness is the forgiving of others. The quality of forgiveness expands even to embrace our "unworthy selves". It is a remarkable process for which we can be truly grateful.[161]

Beginning the work of reviewing our unfinished business needn't wait until death is in view. This is a life skill for today. A way to clear out the dark chambers of our heart, to release our fears and shame and to claim the joy we deserve.

Ars moriendi

Ars moriendi, or 'the art of dying', is an idea handed down from 15th-century Christian literature about how to achieve a 'good death'.

Commissioned by Church authorities at the time of the Council of Constance (1414–1418) the essay, *De arte moriendi*, prescribed a set of prayers, actions and attitudes to help dying people achieve a good death and salvation in the afterlife. The essay was translated into many European languages and became a manual used often by priests in their ministry to the dying.

Today the idea of a good death often finds its expression in notions that everyone has a right to 'die with dignity'. Its chief proposition is that people shouldn't face a protracted or painful dying, or one where they lose control of their body or mind.

Many who support this view say a lingering death is unacceptable, insisting that suicide, euthanasia and medically assisted dying are rights that should be given to anyone who wants to avoid an undignified end. But dying with dignity, whatever it means, also informs some people's choice to refuse further medical treatment in the face of a terminal disease.

Of course, professionals in modern healthcare settings make every effort to prevent and limit the pain and distress endured by dying people and those with terminal medical conditions. And usually, every effort is made to honour people's end-of-life choices expressed in living wills and advance care directives.

But dying is a biological and clinical process with a logic that has no concern for human ideas of dignity. Dying is a series of destructive events that by its nature strips our humanity and obliterates our hopes for dying with dignity. Our desire for dignity dies when the body dies.

For the most part, death doesn't come easily, and our ideas of dignified dying are only compounded by efforts to prevent, conceal, and sanitise dying's momentum. The fact is, most people die in a way they don't want or welcome. Ars moriendi is a fiction rarely seen in emergency rooms, oncology wards and intensive care units.

Rituals of the body

> *I bequeath myself to the dirt*
> *To grow from the grass I love,*
> *If you want me again*
> *Look for me under your boot-soles.*

Walt Whitman [162]

We're not the body, but a lifetime of identifying with the vessel that was animated by life can be a hard habit to break. As humans, we're always and only life itself, briefly occupying a handful of stardust before we're scattered again to the four winds.

What becomes of our body when we cash in our life-deposit needn't preoccupy us but we can demonstrate our love and ease the burden for loved ones by letting them know what we'd like them to do with our corpse.[163] [164] [165]

This matters because they live with the memory of our body. They will live with what they did with it—whether they ignored it, fled from it or embraced it. And what we do with a corpse, we do to ourselves.

Despite appearances, our death needn't end our relationship with the living. If we want, it can be a spur for a conversation that endures beyond our lifetime.

Our body is a reminder that, properly understood, we are deathless. Our life and death are not opposites but the same mystery calling us to union, which means the corpse is a mirror to the living and the dead, not just the dead.

And although we can't ensure that our wishes for our body are honoured, recording them and sharing them is an act of love, a way to care for the living.

Of course, people who are bound in ego-identification will want to control what happens to their body because they believe they are the body. And what happens to their posthumous self is strictly personal, not familial or universal. In death, as in life, they imagine they are still in charge, still calling the shots.

But for anyone with a grander or enlightened sensibility, taking the time to consider and record our wishes for our final days and our post-mortem release is an act of service to our living brethren.

The rituals that accompany dying and the care and disposal of bodies are as diverse as humanity, and there is a growing assortment of services and support for anyone who wants to avail themselves.

Where do you want to die? Who do you want to see in your final days and hours? What kind of support and rituals would you like—music, readings, sensory experiences—as you come to your finale?

You can record these wishes in a 'death plan' and give copies to your family, doctor, executor, and anyone you want to support or carry out your wishes.

In addition to issues such as your will, power of attorney and your advance care directive, a death plan should also cover your wishes for your funeral and what you want done with your body. Sallie Tisdale has an excellent checklist in her helpful book, *Advice for Future Corpses (and Those Who Love Them)*.[166]

The person who decides what happens to your body is your executor. Be sure to choose someone who will honour your wishes, and tell them what you want in person, in your will and in your death plan.

Rather than outsourcing the management of their funeral and burial/cremation to undertakers, many people are joining the growing movement for families to reclaim what what's become the institutionalised care of our dead.

The Natural Death Advocacy Network (NDAN) is an Australian organisation providing resources to help people plan their funeral and what to do with their body when they die. Its areas of advocacy include death education, funeral planning, family-led funeral care, natural burial and bereavement care.

The National Home Funeral Alliance (NHFA) is a US non-profit, volunteer organisation that supports people who want a home funeral. It claims a diverse membership—home funeral guides who also identify as licensed funeral directors, ordained ministers, educators, body workers, social workers, nurses, therapists and counsellors, lawyers and doctors.

'Home funerals are an organic response to the intimate process and aftermath of death, and are as different as the people whose lives they honor,' says the NHFA.

It provides practical information about how to process paperwork, how to care for a body and keep it at home for a few days, how to make and source caskets, urns and shrouds, how to transport a body and make arrangements for 'final disposition', which is code for burial, cremation and alternatives such as sea and sky burials.

*

We are stardust, said the poet. *Billion-year-old carbon*. So how do we *get ourselves back to the garden?* Imagining the disposal and breakdown of our body before we die could be a useful way to break the trance that we are the body, though it's not recommended for anyone alarmed by nature's genius for decomposition and disassembly.

Rituals of the body

Do you want to go into the earth or burn up in smoke? Going into the ground is a surefire way to nurture new life. A rotting corpse is a vessel for a complex ecosystem that emerges soon after death and flourishes as decomposition proceeds.

If you're going into the ground you might want to consider a 'green' or natural burial as a way to harmonise your body with nature.

Green burials are meant to be eco-friendly so that the body goes to the earth in its natural state. This means no toxic chemicals, such as embalming fluid, are used to preserve the body from the point of death. A green burial means the body is commonly placed in a biodegradable container or wrapped in a shroud of linen or silk, and buried without a coffin.

Green burial can mean anything from being buried in your backyard (as long as you follow local law), a conservation reserve, a natural burial ground, or in a hybrid cemetery that provides space for burial without a vault. A natural burial ground can also mean the body is interred with no marker other than a sprouting tree or perhaps a stone.

Cremating or burning the body has a long history and is common around the world. Burning the body at high temperature and then grinding the remains reduces the body to bone fragments and ash. In the West, cremation is usually done in a crematorium but in the Indian subcontinent, especially in India and Nepal, open-air cremation is common.

Why cremation? Some view it as a way of simplifying their funeral process. Others choose it for religious reasons or simply prefer it because it disposes of the body instantly, rather than the slower process of burial and decomposition.

Cremation is not entirely eco-friendly though. According to Wikipedia, each cremation uses about 110 litres of fuel and releases about 240 kg of carbon dioxide into the atmosphere. This means that the one million bodies cremated annually in the United States produce about 240,000 tonnes of carbon dioxide—more CO_2 pollution than 22,000 average American homes generate in a year.

What about turning yourself into compost? Recompose is a US public benefit corporation that will soon provide an alternative to cremation and conventional burial. It offers a process called *recomposition* that converts human remains into soil that can be used for new life.

Recompose says recomposition happens inside a re-usable vessel. Its website says, 'bodies are covered with wood chips and aerated, providing the perfect environment for naturally occurring microbes and beneficial bacteria.'

Recomposition usually takes about 30 days. The company says converting human remains into soil helps minimise waste, avoids polluting groundwater with embalming fluid, and prevents the emission of carbon dioxide emissions arising from cremation and the manufacture of caskets, headstones, and grave liners.

In remote parts of China and Tibet, the custom of 'sky burials' is still done. The body is usually dismembered and laid in the open to be picked over by vultures and scavengers before it goes back to Mother Earth.

Another option is donating yourself to the advancement of forensic anthropology and crime-solving. Some 4,000 people around the world have gifted their body to so-called 'body farms'—research centres that study the decomposition of human remains so criminal investigators and forensic scientists can learn more about how and when people have died in homicides and related circumstances.

The first and most famous of these body farms is based at the

University of Tennessee's Forensic Anthropology Center, in Knoxville, USA. There, scientists assess how bodies change and decompose in a range of circumstances—some buried in shallow graves or floating in a pool, others laid out inside a building or left in the open beneath a tree.

*

In some Zen traditions, students are asked, 'What was your face before you were born?' The question asks students to consider their true nature—that which endures eternally, beyond the transience of the body.[167]

On this point, Stephen Levine says: 'Our original face is our faceless presence. When reflected in the mirror-works of the mind, it is that which experiences thought and feeling. It is the light by which consciousness is lit.

'It peers through the mask of personality and offers life. To discover one's original face is to see behind the mask. Beyond thought and thinking, beyond the known, beyond impermanence, is the ever-present unnamable thusness of being: our timeless, deathless, energetic essence.'[168]

Ars vivendi

Can we achieve anything better than a death-phobic culture's hyped-up hopes of dying with dignity? Or living forever? I think so. Embracing our life and death are opportunities to pursue and celebrate precious mysteries.

Living with an abiding acceptance of our death, be it near or far, is a path for crafting a legacy for our families and loved ones that's almost unimaginable in a death-phobic culture.

Every day we have opportunities to nourish ourselves and those dear to us by cultivating the skills of living and dying well. This matters, because our children and everyone who remembers us will feed at the table we've set.

Sherwin Nuland said the dignity that so many seek in dying is really achieved in the dignity with which we live our lives. *Ars moriendi* is *ars vivendi*.

'The art of dying is the art of living,' he says. 'The honesty and grace of the years of life that are ending is the real measure of how we die. It is not in the last weeks or days that we compose the message that will be remembered, but in all the decades that preceded them. Who has lived in dignity, dies in dignity.'[169]

If we want to make an art of living and dying for ourselves and those we love then we need to learn what these things mean, what they ask of us, and then fashion them from our resources and good intentions.

The bad news is there are no short cuts. The good news is these things can be learned and achieved—but doing so means

Ars vivendi

surrendering a lot of what we think we know about living and dying by expanding our capacity for wonder.

Stephen Jenkinson put it like this: 'Learning wonders about things we claim to know and about knowing at all. It wonders if knowing is all it's cracked up to be. Learning is subversive. What it asks you to pay in tuition is most of what you had thought was true, and what was necessary, and what was enduringly so.'[170]

In this respect, learning how to live and die asks us to learn difficult things that are in short supply: things that can't be downloaded from the internet, wisdom that can't be copy-pasted from books, or readily adapted from TED Talks.

They call for courage and determination and stamina, a willingness to unlearn what we think we need, and a resolution to be in service to something deeply human and long forgotten.

They ask us to live and die with a cognisance of our debt, our inability to repay the bounty given to us, and an intuition for healing our stories of wounding and brokenness, so that we can give the world what it most needs.

Afterword

I didn't expect to live this long but now I've made it to here and the book is done, the last-to-final thing to mention concerns what Paul Kalanithi called *existential authenticity*. The last is to acknowledge the debt of gratitude I owe to the many people who've supported me in this modest writing venture.

But first to Paul Kalanithi, who expressed the inexpressible in his majestic *New York Times* essay (How long have I got left?) from a few years ago.[171] Dr Kalanithi was an Indian-American writer and neurosurgeon who died, aged 37, of stage IV metastatic lung cancer in 2015.

Learning that he had a cancer that kills 70 to 80 per cent of people within two years, he found himself doing what many of us do when given a death sentence—he sought certainty where there is none.

Poignantly, he understood his dilemma from both sides—as a doctor and patient. As a doctor, he'd been careful to be honest but suitably vague about giving his patients a prognosis, while trying to offer a glimmer of hope. He would use phrases like 'days to weeks, weeks to months, months to a few years,' knowing most patients would Google survival numbers in a bid to fill the anxiety gap between medical opinion and the idiosyncrasies of individual disease progression.

So, when his diagnosis came, he too asked his doctor—a world expert in lung cancer—how long he had to live, hoping she would see him as someone who understood medical statistics and the grim facts of his disease. She refused point blank to give him a

Afterword

number and suddenly, despite being her medical colleague and an esteemed neurosurgeon, he was forced to begin his descent into the powerlessness and uncertainty of being a terminal patient. There was no cure. All he could do was ask questions and adapt his remaining life to changing circumstances.

His reading told him he might have weeks, months, years—maybe two, maybe ten. But nothing was certain and the unexpected twist was this: facing the fact that he had a disease that would kill him changed everything but changed nothing.

Before cancer, he knew he'd die one day but didn't know when. After cancer, he knew he'd die one day but didn't know when, only now he knew it *acutely*. It was like the Zen riddle of enlightenment: 'Before enlightenment, chop wood, carry water. After enlightenment, chop wood, carry water.'

Kalanithi didn't know whether to make funeral arrangements, write the book he'd planned, or carry on being a doctor. What he came to, eventually, was that knowing how much time he had remaining wouldn't remedy the terror he felt in squarely facing death—not later, but today, if necessary.

Would he submit to mortality? Would he bow to transience while seeking a way to 'go on' when going on was impossible? Would he abandon hope and navigate towards existential authenticity, knowing he could be blown off course, smashed to oblivion, and drowned before he found land? Would he find his lotus before winter?[172]

Sooner or later, this is the journey we're all called to. For some it comes in the form of a 'health scare' like an abnormal pap smear or high PSA test result. Others get it when they witness a tragedy like a fatal motor vehicle accident at close quarters. Some get the news in the form of a genetic test indicating an elevated risk for a deadly or degenerative brain disease.

Mine was cancer, and the writing of these essays, which began before my diagnosis, has leavened my life in a way that meant the *writing* became the end I sought, not completing the essays or publishing them.

This was wholly unexpected. I'd set sail in fear and ignorance—ignorant of my deeper motives and fearful that I had nothing original to add to the vast literature on the sociology of death, dying and an examined life.

But I was determined to say something, damn it, because my reading of what might be called the literature of 'living and dying well', while uplifting, still left me feeling oddly dissatisfied. In the past 30 years, writers like Sherwin Nuland, Elisabeth Kübler-Ross, Joan Didion, William Thomas, Stephen Levine, Stephen Jenkinson and Atul Gawande have torn away the secrecy and shibboleths that shroud dying and death trades. They've transformed the way many of us think and feel about death and dying, and how we want our demise and deaths to be.

But I needed more—authors who could write with what Walt Whitman called a 'physiological-spiritual' sensibility. Writers steeped in philosophy, literature, science, mythology and spirituality. Practitioners who were getting their hands dirty trying to manifest their learning in their lives and the lives of others. People who were walking the talk.

So, I appointed myself to the task in the knowledge that I was vastly unqualified yet determined to record the soul work of a life in progress, maybe an elder-in-making, while time and health allowed. By contrast, Paul Kalanithi was vastly better informed—a scholar of literature and philosophy, an expert neurosurgeon, literally dying as he penned his final opus.

But having decided to write, all I could rightly do was read. And the more I read, the less sure I was that I could say anything

Afterword

intelligent or worthwhile. Besides, the literature of death and an examined life was peopled with giants: Sophocles, Rumi, Shakespeare, Montaigne, Freud, Jung, Tolstoy, Campbell, Dickinson, Whitman, Thoreau, Nietzsche, Faulkner and Krishnamurti, to name a few.

In reading the titans, whom I'd barely visited since university days, it dawned that my reading was both my soul work and a reacquaintance with wisdom that might inform a writing venture informed by Whitman's physiological-spiritual sensibility.

When this crystallised, my reading and the early drafts began to fuse with authentic purpose. They became my medicine and opened my heart. Eventually, I found the target of this self-medication was my fractured life. I was still in pieces, begging for someone else to 'mend my life', as Mary Oliver put it.

And one phrase kept returning to haunt and inspire: 'Today is a good day to die for all the things of my life are present.' Attributed to the Oglala Lakota chief Low Dog, who fought with Sitting Bull against US General Custer's troops at the Battle of Little Bighorn in 1876.

For me, the adage embodies the prospect of living life with an open-hearted immediacy that accepts death at any moment, a death uncrowded by fears, regrets or denials. Living in the knowledge that death is our constant companion: that it can claim us at any moment, and that we are ready for it.[173][174] A life freely running to its closure here, and opening, with a 'shout of joy, there'.[175]

Acknowledgments

To the following people I owe a large debt of gratitude. Professor Stephen Larsen, thank you for restoring my life through your unfailing humanity and expert medical care. May our collaboration continue.

Anne Blair-Hickman: thank you for listening, believing and encouraging with such generosity. Your love spurs and sustains me.

Garth Alley for guiding me home. You're the constant, the axis mundi with a warm and curious heart.

Heather Millar of Zest Communications, thank you for expertly editing the manuscript. You brought a sharp eye, sage advice and warm wit to the venture. My tangled prose is clearer, more cogent and more personal thanks to you.

John Duffy, the best friend in the world. Thanks for holding my feet to the fire with love and compassion.

Shaun Stevenson, for grace and love, and pointing the way, all those years ago. Your example as a father and fellow traveller inspire me.

John Gaughan, for mentoring my humanity.

Dennis Shackley, for inspiring me to be the man I could be, and persevering after all these years.

Denis Fitzpatrick for true grit and leading the way to elderhood.

Lisa Gorman, a wise and warm co-conspirator in the project of how to live a life of value and meaning.

Murray Hopkins, a gifted and generous elder who teaches me how to live an examined life.

Acknowledgments

Vicky Puig, for soul, and showing me what it looks like to live in connected community and enlightened love.

Good Samaritan Sister Joy Edwards, a pioneer, a mentor and the last great elder of our tribe, who prays for me every day.

And the late, great John Peace, CP: comrade, friend and cousin who bore witness to his faith and changed the world for the better through his infinite love and service.

Resources and inspiration

The Death Letter Project
Tina FiveAsh, 2017
What is death? What happens when we die? Fifty Australians were invited to write a letter responding to these two questions.

How to prepare for a good death
Dr BJ Miller, IDEAS.TED.COM, 2015
Wise words and solid advice from BJ Miller, who thinks deeply about the end of life as head of the Zen Hospice Project.

Falling Into Grace: Insights on the End of Suffering
Adyashanti, Sounds True, 2011
A crystal clear account of why we suffer and how to end suffering by waking up from the illusion that we are a separate self.

Last Acts of Kindness: Lessons for the Living from the Bedsides of the Dying
Judith Redwing Keyssar, CreateSpace Independent Publishing, 2010
When Plato was asked to sum up his life's work, he said, 'practice dying.' Last Acts of Kindness provides a glimpse into this practice through the stories of those who have lived and died.

The Four Things That Matter Most: A Book About Living
Ira Byock, Atria, 2014
Stories from people who have turned to this life-altering book in their time of need. This book about what really matters reminds us how we can honour each relationship every day.

Resources and inspiration

The Ultimate Journey: Consciousness and the Mystery of Death
Stanislav Grof, Multidisciplinary Association for Psychedelic Studies, 2006
A book that draws on old wisdom and modern science to reveal the significance of birth and death.

Alive Inside (film)
Michael Rossato-Bennett, Ximotion Media, 2013
A joyful cinematic examination of music's capacity to awaken our souls and probe our humanity.

Extemis (film)
Dan Krauss, Netflix, 2016
An extraordinary documentary that reveals the devastation experienced by three dying patients and their families because they didn't speak up sooner about life and death choices.

Consider the Seed
Shozan Jack Haubner, Tricycle Magazine, Fall 2013
Reflecting on our cosmic origins, a wayward monk reveals how nature demands that we must die in order to grow.

Zen Mind, Beginner's Mind
Shunryu Suzuki, Weatherhill Inc, 1970
A popular and easy-to-read book on Zen and Buddhism in the West.

Death's Summer Coat: What the History of Death and Dying Can Tell Us About Life and Living
Brandy Schillace, Pegasus Books, 2016
An absorbing exploration of the history of death and dying and the rituals that surround it, this book examines the many ways that humans have dealt with mortality throughout history.

When Breath Becomes Air
Paul Kalanithi, Random House 2016
A life-affirming reflection about facing death and the relationship between being a doctor and patient, by a gifted writer who became both. Neurosurgeon and father, Paul Kalanithi died at age 37 while working on this profoundly moving book.

Death Is Hard Work
Khaled Khalifa, Faber & Faber, 2019
An old man dies in a hospital bed in Damascus but tells his youngest son, Bolbol, his final wish is to be buried in the family plot in their ancestral village in the Aleppo region. Bolbol and his estranged siblings embark on an odyssey through war-ravaged Syria to honour their father's wish. Hard Work is an unforgettable journey into a contemporary heart of darkness.

No Mud, No Lotus: The Art of Transforming Suffering
Thich Nhat Hanh, Parallax Press, 2015
The secret to happiness lies in recognising and transforming our suffering, rather that running from it. Zen master, Thich Nhat Hanh recommends practices such as stopping, mindful breathing, and deep concentration to foster mindfulness so that we can be in touch with our suffering without being overwhelmed by it.

Credits

Brief quote from p16 from *The Tibetan Book of Living and Dying* by Sogyol Rinpoche, edited by Patrick Gaffney and Andrew Harvey, copyright © 1993 by Rigpa Fellowship, reprinted by permission of HarperCollins Publishers.

Excerpts from pages 20, 21, 35, 117-118, 121, 168, 217, 250, 283-284 from *Die Wise: A Manifesto for Sanity and Soul* by Stephen Jenkinson, published by North Atlantic Books, copyright © 2015 by Stephen Jenkinson. Reprinted by permission of North Atlantic Books.

Excerpts from *How We Die: Reflections on Life's Final Chapter* by Sherwin B. Nuland, copyright © 1994 by Sherwin B Nuland. Used by permission of Alfred A Knopf, an imprint of the Knopf Doubleday Publishing Group, a division of Penguin Random House LLC. All rights reserved.

Excerpt by Stephen Jay Gould from *Bully for Brontosaurus: Reflections in Natural History*, New York: W W Norton & Company, 1991. Used with permission. The passage was originally published by SJ Gould in a paper titled *The median isn't the message.* Discover 6 (June): 40–42.

Excerpt by Stephen Jenkinson from The *Meaning of Death, Orphan Wisdom* (2013) used with permission of the publisher and author.

Excerpt by Stephen Jenkinson from *The Making of Humans, Orphan Wisdom* (2014) used with permission of the publisher and author.

Excerpt(s) from pages 1, 14-15, 82-83, 83-84 and p159 from *A Year to Live: How to Live This Year as if it Were Your Last* by Stephen Levine, copyright © 1997 by Stephen Levine. Used by permission of Bell Tower, an imprint of the Crown Publishing Group, a division of Penguin Random House LLC. All rights reserved.

Excerpt by Garrard, E and Wrigley, A (2009) Hope and terminal illness: false hope versus absolute hope. *Clinical Ethics*, March 4(1). Licensed with permission of SAGE Publications RightsLink, licence number 4353870436554.

Excerpt by Bryan Schatz, The Amazing Story Behind Syria's Miracle Baby, *Vocativ*, 16 December 2014 used with permission of the author.

'Tilicho Lake' used with permission of the author, David Whyte, and publisher, Many Rivers Press.

Excerpt by Miller, BJ (2015). What really matters at the end of life. *TED Talk*, March used under Creative Commons.

Excerpt by Ensler, E (2004). The Pursuit of Happiness, *TED Talk*, Monterey, California, 25-28 February used under Creative Commons.

Excerpt quoting Edgar Mitchell in the documentary, *In the Shadow of the Moon* (2007) used with permission of director, David Sington.

Excerpts from *The Masks of God: Primitive Mythology, Volume 1* by Joseph Campbell, copyright © 1959, 1969, renewed © 1987 by Joseph Campbell. Used by permission of Viking Books, an imprint of Penguin Publishing Group, a division of Penguin Random House LLC. All rights reserved.

Excerpts from *The Masks of God: Primitive Mythology, Volume 1* by Joseph Campbell, copyright © 1972 by Joseph Campbell. Used

Credits

by permission of the Joseph Campbell Foundation in the UK and Commonwealth. All rights reserved.

'Circle of Breath' used with permission of the publisher, Graywolf Press.

Quote from palliative care expert, Professor Kate White, Professor of Susan Wakil School of Nursing and Midwifery, University of Sydney, used with permission.

Quote from Dr Linda Sheahan, Staff Specialist Palliative Medicine, Clinical Ethics Consultant SESLHD, Honorary Associate, Sydney Health Ethics, University of Sydney, Conjoint SPHCM UNSW, Affiliated Ethicist, Joint Centre for Bioethics, University of Toronto, Canada, used with permission.

The Complete Essays by Michel de Montaigne, translated with an introduction and notes by M. A. Screech, published by Penguin Books. With permission from Penguin Books Ltd. Copyright © M. A. Screech, 1987, 1991.

Excerpts from *Being Mortal – Illness, Medicine and What Matters in the End,* Profile Books, p155 and 173 granted with permission within fair use limits in the UK and Commonwealth.

Endnotes

[1] *The Diamond Sutra*. (868AD), British Library

[2] Jenkinson, S (2014) *Die Wise: A Manifesto for Sanity and Soul*. North Atlantic Books, Berkeley, California, p35

[3] Gawande, A (2014). *Being Mortal – Illness, Medicine and What Matters in the End*, Profile Books, p173

[4] Horsfall, D, Noonan, K and Leonard, R. (2012). Bringing our dying home: how caring for someone at the end of life builds social capital and builds compassionate communities. *Health Sociology Review*, 21(4), pp 373–382

[5] Tisdale, S (2018). *Advice for Future Corpses: a practical perspective on death and dying*, Allen and Unwin, p50

[6] Jenkinson, S (2013). *The Meaning of Death*, Orphan Wisdom

[7] Ibid

[8] Levine, S (1997). *A Year to Live*, Bell Tower, p159

[9] Brooks, D (2019). The Moral Peril of Meritocracy, *The New York Times*, April 6

[10] Ness, R (2017). Wisdom and altruism come with age. *Houston Chronicle*, February 6

[11] Nuland, SB (1995). *How We Die: Reflections on Life's Final Chapter*. Epub, Vintage Books, Random House, New York, p13

[12] Connor, SR et al (2007). Comparing hospice and non-hospice patient survival among patients who die within a three-year window. *Journal of Pain and Symptom Management*, 33, pp 238-246

[13] Temel, JS et al (2010). Early Palliative Care for Patients with Metastatic Non–Small-Cell Lung Cancer. *New England Journal of Medicine*, 363, pp 33-42

[14] NSW Cancer Plan, Cancer Institute NSW, Sydney, April 2016

[15] Gould, SJ (1985). The Median Isn't the Message. *Discover*, 6 (June), pp 40–42

[16] White, K (2015). *Dying Well, Professor Kate White, University of Sydney*, YouTube, September 13

[17] Djulbegovic, BJ et al (2012). New treatments compared to established treatments in randomized trials. *Cochrane Database Syst. Rev*, 10: MR000024

[18] Djulbegovic, BJ et al (2013). Treatment Success in Cancer: Industry Compared to Publicly Sponsored Randomized Controlled Trials. *PLoS ONE*, 8, e58711

[19] Djulbegovic, BJ et al (2012). Op cit

[20] Jenkinson, S (2014). Ibid, p217

[21] Jenkinson, S (2000). *Money and the Soul's Desires*. Stoddart

[22] Kalanithi, P (2016). How long have I got left? *The New York Times*, January 24

[23] AIHW (2014) *Cancer in Australia: an overview 2014*. Cancer series no. 90, Cat. no CAN 88, Canberra

[24] Department of Human Services (2017). *Pharmaceutical Benefits Scheme—Complex Drugs*, letter, November 29

[25] Commonwealth Department of Health (2018). Dr John Paul, Secretary, *Pharmaceutical Benefits Advisory Committee*, letter, January 18

[26] Ibid

[27] Department of Human Services (2017). Op cit

[28] Power, J (2018). Terminal cancer patient denied access to life-extending chemo drug. *The Sydney Morning Herald*, February 24

[29] McKenna, J (2016). *Dreamstate: A Conspiracy Theory*, Wisefool Press, p55

[30] McKenna, J (2010). *Spiritual Enlightenment: The Damnedest Thing*, Wisefool Press

[31] Martin, CE (2015). Zen and the Art of Dying Well. *The New York Times*, August 14

[32] Mooallem, J (2017). One Man's Quest to Change the Way We Die. *The New York Times*, January 3

[33] Jenkinson, S (2014). Op cit, p35

[34] Miller, BJ (2015). What really matters at the end of life. *TED Talk*, March. For more TED content, visit ted.com

[35] Smith, NM (2016). Other People review: cancer comedy lets Molly Shannon wring all types of tears, *The Guardian*, January 23

[36] Gawande, A (2014). *Being Mortal – Illness, Medicine and What Matters in the End*, Profile Books, p155

[37] Sheahan, L (2015), *Dying well—Dr Linda Sheahan, palliative care medical specialist*, YouTube, October 8

[38] Cave, S (2012*). Immortality: The Quest to Live Forever and How It Drives Civilization*, Crown

[39] Motoko, R (2010). For the Unemployed Over 50, Fears of Never

Working Again, *The New York Times*, September 19

[40] Jefferson, T (1814) Letter to John Adams, July 5. *The Letters of Thomas Jefferson, 1743-1826*

[41] Kelly Scientific Publications (2015) *Global Cosmetic Surgery and Service Market Report 2015-2019*

[42] Martin, GM (1982). Syndromes of accelerated aging. *National Cancer Institute Monograph*; 60: 241-7

[43] F. Gonzalez-Crussi (1987). *Three Forms of Sudden Death: And Other Reflections on the Grandeur and Misery of the Body*, Picador Books, p27

[44] Jenkinson, S (2018). *Come of Age: The Case for Elderhood in a Time of Trouble*, North Atlantic Books. Kindle Edition, p43

[45] Devlin, H (2017). Life on Mars: Elon Musk reveals details of his colonisation vision, *The Guardian*, June 16

[46] PBS documentary (1988). *Joseph Campbell and the Power of Myth*, episode 4

[47] Rustoen, T. (1995). Hope and quality of life, two central issues for cancer patients: a theoretical analysis. *Cancer Nursing*, 18(5), pp 355–361.

[48] Ferrell, BR and Coyle, N, eds (2005). *Textbook of Palliative Nursing*. (2nd ed). Oxford: Oxford University Press

[49] Garrard, E and Wrigley, A (2009) Hope and terminal illness: false hope versus absolute hope. *Clinical Ethics*, 4(1), p38

[50] Nicholas, A et al (2000). Extent and determinants of error in doctors' prognoses in terminally ill patients: prospective cohort study. *BMJ*, 320, pp 469-73

[51] Weeks JC, et al (1998). Relationship between cancer patients' predictions of prognosis and their treatment preferences. *JAMA*,

279, pp 1709-14

[52] Jenkinson, S (2014). Op cit, p121

[53] Bowler, K (2018). How Cancer Changes Hope. *The New York Times*, December 28

[54] Goldstein, J (2008). Cause and Effect: Reflecting on the law of karma. *Tricycle Magazine*

[55] Thich Nhat, H (2015). *No Mud, No Lotus: The Art of Transforming Suffering*, Parallax Press

[56] Tolle, E (2004). *The Power of Now: a guide to spiritual enlightenment*. Hachette Australia

[57] Gotink RA et al (2015). Standardised Mindfulness-Based Interventions in Healthcare: An Overview of Systematic Reviews and Meta-Analyses of RCTs. *PLOS ONE*, 10 (4)

[58] Goyal, M et al. (2014). Meditation Programs for Psychological Stress and Well-being: A Systematic Review and Meta-analysis. *JAMA Internal Medicine*, 174 (3), pp 357–68

[59] Nuland, SB (1995). Op cit, p148

[60] Nuland, SB (1995) Op cit, p170

[61] Eliot, TS (1922). *The Waste Land*. New York: Horace Liveright

[62] Eisenstein, C (2013). *The More Beautiful World Our Hearts Know Is Possible*. North Atlantic Books, Scarcity (ch 18)

[63] PBS documentary (1988). *Joseph Campbell and the Power of Myth*, episode 2

[64] Jenkinson, S (2013). *Time is religion: The Haiku Sessions*. Orphan Wisdom

[65] Lovelock, JE (1972). Gaia as seen through the atmosphere. *Atmospheric Environment*; 6(8): 579–580

[66] Jenkinson, S (2014). Op cit, p2

[67] Jenkinson, S (2018). Op cit, p293-297

[68] Hesse, H (2018). *Siddhartha*, Penguin Books, London, United Kingdom

[69] PBS documentary (1988). Op cit, episode 2

[70] Shakespeare, W. *As You Like It*, Act II, Scene VII: The Concise Oxford Companion to English Literature (3rd ed), 2013: Margaret Drabble, Jenny Stringer, Daniel Hann. Oxford University Press

[71] Levine, S (1997). *A Year to Live*, Bell Tower, p40

[72] Levine, S (1997). Ibid, p1

[73] Levine, S (1997). Ibid, pp 14-15

[74] Castle Rock Entertainment (2007). *The Bucket List*

[75] McKenna, J (2016). Op cit, p47

[76] McKenna, J (2016). Op cit, p85

[77] Stafford, W (2014). 'Circle of Breath' from *Ask Me: 100 essential poems*. Edited by Kim Stafford, Graywolf Press

[78] International Union for Conservation of Nature (2015). *The IUCN Red List of Threatened Species*

[79] Intergovernmental Science-Policy Platform on Biodiversity and Ecosystem Services (2019). *Global Assessment of Biodiversity and Ecosystem Services*, May 6

[80] Plumer, B (2019). Humans Are Speeding Extinction and Altering the Natural World at an 'Unprecedented' Pace, *The New York Times*, May 6

[81] Pimm, SL et al (2014). The biodiversity of species and their rates of extinction, distribution, and protection. *Science*, 344, 6187

[82] Zhang, S (2015). Nola the Northern White Rhino's Death Leaves Just Three on Earth. *Wired*, November 23

[83] Mazza, E (2015). Nola, one of the world's last Northern White Rhinos has died. *The Huffington Post*, November 22

[84] San Diego Zoo (2015). Nola, the Northern White Rhino leaves an immeasurable legacy through her contributions to science. November 24

[85] Jenkinson, S (2014). Op cit, p21

[86] Levine, S (1997). Op cit, pp 149-150

[87] Joint science academies' statement (2014). *Global response to climate change*. January 6

[88] Stocker, TF et al (2013). Climate Change 2013: The Physical Science Basis. Working Group 1. *5th Assessment Report*, IPCC

[89] Monbiot, G (2016) *How Did We Get Into This Mess?* Verso Books

[90] Adamson, R. The Indian Giver (1991) cited in Berry, M and Adamson, R (2000). *The Wisdom of the Giveaway – A Guide to Growing Native American Philanthropy*. Center on Philanthropy and Civil Society at The Graduate Center, City University of New York, pp 1-2

[91] Jenkinson, S (2014). Op cit, p20

[92] Wallace-Wells, D (2019). *The Uninhabitable Earth: Life After Warming*, Tim Duggan Books.

[93] Robinson, M (2014). Animal Personhood in Mi'kmaq Perspective. *Societies* 4(4), pp 672-688

[94] Dargis, M (2009). Meet Your New Farmer: Hungry Corporate Giant. *The New York Times*, June 11

[95] Jenkinson, S (2014). Op cit, pp 117-118

[96] Armstrong, K (2005). *A Short History of Myth*. Text Publishing Company, pp 5-6

[97] Jenkinson, S (2018). Op cit, pp 196-197

[98] Thorpe, L (2012). *A Study of Modern Day Slavery*. International Disciples of Women's Ministries of the Christian Church

[99] Clarkson, L et al (1992). *Our Responsibility to The Seventh Generation: Indigenous Peoples and Sustainable Development*. International Institute for Sustainable Development, Winnipeg

[100] Jenkinson, S (2018), Op cit, pp 204-205

[101] Australian Human Rights Commission (1997). *Bringing Them Home: Report of the National Inquiry into the Separation of Aboriginal and Torres Strait Islander Children from Their Families*

[102] Jenkinson, S (2014). Op cit, p250

[103] Vass, A et al (1992). Time since death determinations of human cadavers using soil solution. *Journal of Forensic Sciences*, 37 (5), pp 1236–1253

[104] Anderson B (2013). Dynamics of ninhydrin-reactive nitrogen and pH in grave soil during the extended postmortem interval. *Journal of Forensic Science*, Sept 58(5)

[105] Oliver, M (2013). *A Thousand Mornings*, Penguin Books, pp27-28

[106] Fitzherbert, Y (2015). Abdullah Kurdi: The long return to Kobane. *Middle Eastern Eye*, September 8

[107] Hopper, T (2015). The sad odyssey of Alan Kurdi and his family: Their search for new life ended in death. *National Post*, September 3

[108] Glavin, T (2015). Why little Alan Kurdi and his family never really had a chance of reaching Canada. *National Post*, September 3

[109] Kuntz, K (2015). 'I Feel like I Am Dead': Alan Kurdi's Father Tells His Story, *Der Spiegel*, September 14

[110] Wikipedia (2015). Death of Alan Kurdi

[111] UNHCR (2015). *Global Trends Report: Forced Displacements*

[112] Australia for UNHCR (2015). *Refugee Crisis in Europe*

[113] Associated Press (2015). Over 1 million refugees, migrants estimated to have entered Europe this year. December 22

[114] Barnard, A (2019). Inside Syria's Secret Torture Prisons: How Bashar al-Assad Crushed Dissent, *The New York Times*, May 11

[115] Shear, MD, Kanno-Youngs, Z (2019). Trump administration to push for tougher Asylum rules. *The New York Times*, April 9

[116] Adyashanti (2011). *Falling Into Grace: Insights on the End of Suffering*. Sounds True Inc, Boulder CO

[117] Revkin, AC (2014) In Urbanization Update, U.N. Sees Tokyo Atop Megacities List Until 2030, *The New York Times*, July 10

[118] Rinpoche, S (2008). *The Tibetan Book of Living and Dying*, edited by Patrick Gaffney and Andrew Harvey, Rigpa Fellowship, HarperCollins Publishers

[119] Farah, K (2016). *White Helmets*. Grain Media; Violet Films; North Kivu Film Productions

[120] Schatz, B (2014). The Amazing Story Behind Syria's Miracle Baby, *Vocativ*, December 16

[121] Farah, K (2016). Ibid

[122] Omar, A (2016). Op cit

[123] Jenkinson, S (2014). *The Making of Humans*, Orphan Wisdom

[124] Campbell, JJ (1991). *The Masks of God Volume 1: Primitive Mythology*. Viking Penguin, p66

[125] Khalifa, K (2019). *Death is Hard Work*. ebook translated from Arabic to English by Leri Price, Faber and Faber

[126] Michel de Montaigne, *The Essays of Michel de Montaigne*, translated and edited by MA Screech (London: Allen Lane, 1991), p95.

[127] Letters (2019), When Bat Mitzvahs Are More Spectacle Than Spiritual. *The New York Times*, May 2

[128] Ross, G (2013) Muslim activists: Fight extreme materials online with counter messages. *CIO*, May 28

[129] Seccombe, M (2015). The vexed power of the Grand Mufti. *The Saturday Paper*, 28 November–3 December, p10

[130] White, D (2012). *River Flow: New and Selected Poems*, Revised Edition, Many Rivers Press

[131] Mitchell, E (2007). *In the Shadow of the Moon*, documentary film, director, David Sington

[132] Ibid, p109

[133] Rinpoche, S (2008). Op cit, p16.

[134] Tolle, E (2004). Op cit

[135] Ensler, E (2000). *The Vagina Monologues*, Dramatists Play Service Inc

[136] Ensler, E (2004). *Happiness in body and soul*, TED Talk, Monterey, California, February. For more TED content, visit ted.com

[137] Van Erp, S and Verstricht, L (2008). Longing in a Culture of Cynicism: Introductory essay by David Tracy: *On longing, the Void, The Open God*. LIT Verlag Münster

[138] Ensler, E (2004). Op cit

[139] Jenkinson, S (2013). *Water of Forgetting, The Haiku Sessions*. Orphan Wisdom

[140] Londoño, E (2017), In Rio de Janeiro, 'Complete Vulnerability' as Violence Surges, *The New York Times*, November 18

[141] Graham-McLay, C (2019), Death Toll in New Zealand Mosque Shootings Rises to 51, *The New York Times*, May 2

[142] Rojas, R (2019), New York Archdiocese Names 120 Catholic Clergy Members Accused of Abuse, *The New York Times*, April 26

[143] Thich Nhat, H (2015). Op cit

[144] Keown, K (2013). *Buddhism: A Very Short Introduction*, Oxford University Press, pp 48–62

[145] Puri, S (2019). The Lesson of Impermanence, *The New York Times*, March 9

[146] Wright AA et al (2008). Associations between end-of-life discussions, patient mental health, medical care near death, and caregiver bereavement adjustment. *JAMA*, 300(14), pp 1665–1673

[147] Gostin LO (2014). Legal and Ethical Responsibilities Following Brain Death: The McMath and Muñoz Cases. *JAMA*, 311(9), pp 903-904

[148] Juahar, S (2019). What is Death? *The New York Times*, 16 February

[149] NSW Ministry of Health (November 2018). *Making an Advance Care Directive*, ISBN 978-1-76000-996-0

[150] Jenkinson, S (2014). Op cit, p168

[151] Quill, TE and Battin, MP, editors (2004). *Physician-assisted dying: the case for palliative care and patient choice*. Baltimore, Md., Johns Hopkins University Press

[152] Pearlman, RA et al (2005). *J Gen Intern Med*. Mar; 20(3): 234–239

[153] Jenkinson, S (2018). Op cit, p2

[154] Sacred Congregation for the Doctrine of the Faith (May 5, 1980). *Declaration on Euthanasia*

[155] Maria Sacchetti, M and Guskin, E (2017). In rural America, fewer immigrants and less tolerance, *The Washington Post*, June 17

[156] Staff (2018). A timescale for the origin and evolution of all of life on Earth. *Phys.org*, 20 August

[157] Vanguard (2018). The global financial crisis: Behind us but far from over, September 28

[158] Jenkinson, S (2018), op cit, pp 262-263

[159] Levine, S (1997). Op cit, pp 69-70

[160] Levine, S (1997). Op cit, pp 82-83

[161] Levine, S (1997). Op cit, pp 83-84

[162] Whitman, W. *Leaves of Grass* (1855). The Walt Whitman Archive. Edited by Ed Folsom and Kenneth M Price

[163] Tisdale, S (2018). Op cit, p156

[164] Browne, K. What to do when someone dies, *Choice*

[165] Commonwealth Government of Australia. *What to do following a death.* Department of Human Services

[166] Tisdale, S (2018). Op Cit, Appendix 1

[167] Suzuki, S (1970). *Zen Mind, Beginner's Mind*, Weatherhill Inc

[168] Levine, S (1997). Op cit, p118

[169] Nuland, S (1995). Op cit, p172

[170] Jenkinson, S (2014). Op cit, pp 283-84

[171] Kalanithi, P (2016). How long have I got left? *The New York Times*, January 24

[172] Levine, S (1997). Op cit, p150

[173] Cited by Richard G Hardorff, editor (2004). *Indian Views of the Custer Fight: A source book*, chapter 6: The Low Dog Interview, AH Clark Company, pp 63-66. Excerpt originally published in *Leavenworth Times*, 14 August 1881

[174] Levine, S (1997) *Op cit*, pp 154-155

[175] Barks, C (2001). *The Soul of Rumi*, 'On the Day I Die'. HarperCollins Publishers Inc, p94

www.ingramcontent.com/pod-product-compliance
Lightning Source LLC
Chambersburg PA
CBHW051946290426
44110CB00015B/2130